FINDING A LOVING GOD IN THE MIDST OF GRIEF

SUSAN M. ERSCHEN

the WORD
among us®
press

Published by The Word Among Us Press
7115 Guilford Drive, Suite 100
Frederick, Maryland 21704
wau.org

23 22 21 20 19 1 2 3 4 5

ISBN: 978-1-59325-346-2
eISBN: 978-1-59325-532-9

Cover design by Faceout Studios

Made and printed in the United States of America

Library of Congress Control Number: 2019935450

CONTENTS

Author's Note

Dear Reader,

Here is the most important thing I know about grief: it's a different journey for each of us.

We all eventually visit most of the same spots, but we don't do it in the same order. For example, deciding what to keep of our loved one's things and what to give away might be an immediate need for practical or emotional reasons. For others, this step might wait for months.

Some will find that forgiveness is an essential stop early in the journey. For others, forgiveness might be the very last place they visit.

This truth about our grief journeys made it difficult for me to decide the order of the chapters in this book. The best I could do for you is to make sure each chapter stood on its own. So please feel free to read these chapters in whatever order is most helpful for you. You can skip a chapter if you're not ready for it, or you can jump ahead to something you feel you need sooner rather than later. Let the Spirit guide you to what you need from these pages.

I am most sorry for your loss. I have prayed for you as I have written this book, and I hope it brings you comfort.

God bless!
Sue Erschen

CHAPTER 1

Natural but Unique

I walked away from my dad's graveside service, crying unashamedly. The final prayers, the gun salute, and the presentation of the flag for this World War II veteran were more than my fragile emotions could handle. I hugged and was hugged by my husband, my children, my brother, and my sisters. All of us shared a deep and overwhelming grief at that moment.

Then my four-year-old grandson was beside me, tugging at my hand. "Grandma," he asked, with great concern on his face, "are you always going to be sad?" Clearly my tears were upsetting to him. He had probably never seen me cry before.

I smiled down at him and assured him, "No, I won't always be sad. But I do need to be sad for a little while. Okay?"

Different for Each of Us

How long will this last? This is a question we ask when we are grieving or when someone close to us is grieving. How long will we cry at the slightest thing? How long will we feel disconnected from life, angry, listless, or anxious? There are no dependable answers for these questions.

The ancients asked this question too.

> How long, LORD? Will you utterly forget me?
>   How long will you hide your face from me?
> How long must I carry sorrow in my soul,
>   grief in my heart day after day? (Psalm 13:2-3)

1

Many of the prophets repeated the same lament. Even today we cannot accurately answer the question of how long grief will last or what it will look like. It is different for everyone.

Some people can overcome the worst of grief in just a few weeks. For most of us, it may take six months to a year. Yet many people will have recurring episodes of grief for years after the loss. The goal is not to recover from grief as quickly as possible but rather to recover *well*. The longer we deny our feeling of grief, the longer it will take for us to fully recover.

Over the years, some experts have tried to put a timeline on grief. We often hear that it will take a year. One must go through every holiday, birthday, anniversary, and special day at least once. But this isn't always true. Some find the second year harder than the first, and others move forward in less than a year.

In the last half of the twentieth century, Dr. Elisabeth Kübler-Ross, in her landmark book *On Death and Dying,* put forth the theory that people had to go through five stages of grief: denial, anger, bargaining, depression, and acceptance. But today many grief counselors disavow this theory. They say people experience different symptoms of grief at different times, and expecting a grieving person to follow a certain pattern can only hamper the process.

The simple fact is that everyone grieves differently. There is no right or wrong way. Grief is an extremely personal experience that can be influenced by many circumstances. The timing of the death, the way the person died, and other stress in our lives at the time can all impact how we grieve. Grief is difficult enough without adding the additional burden of judgment. When we face grief, we need to take Our Lord's words to heart: "Stop judging, that you may not be judged" (Matthew 7:1). We should never judge anyone for the way they are grieving. Nor should we let anyone judge us.

Everyone Grieves

One thing we know for sure is that everyone grieves at some time. As much as death is a part of life, grief is also a part of life. Inevitably, when one person dies, another one will grieve. Yet we like to ignore grief, push it under the carpet, pretend that it isn't there. Take your three or four days of bereavement time, and then please get back to work. Don't mention it again.

However, ignoring grief isn't helpful. It's not healthy to pretend our grief disappeared in a week and that everything is back to normal. When we lose someone we love, grief will be with us for a while. It will change us in many ways. We will find our way through our grief more easily if we accept grieving as a good and instinctive process. It's a natural side effect of loving.

We may ask, "If God loves me, why would he make me go through this?" Yet even people closest to God knew great and overwhelming grief. Scripture is full of grief.

- Naomi, in the Old Testament Book of Ruth, was stranded in a foreign land after her husband and her two sons died.
- Job lost his entire family.

- Jacob spent a lifetime grieving the loss of his dear son Joseph, who had been sold to Egyptian traders.
- The mother of Jesus watched as her only son was tortured to death.
- The apostle John stood at the cross with Mary and saw his best friend suffer and die.
- St. Mary Magdalene was torn with grief as she wandered the garden on Easter Sunday.
- The two disciples on the road to Emmaus were grieving the loss of an inspiring teacher.

Great people in recent centuries too have experienced profound grief.

- St. Elizabeth Ann Seton buried her beloved husband while she was still a young woman with five small children. The way she handled this great grief has made her a patron saint for all those who grieve.
- St. Thérèse of Lisieux lost her mother when she was four and her father when she was twenty-one.
- Christian writer C. S. Lewis filled all the notebooks in his house journaling about his grief when his wife died.
- Pope St. John the XXIII grieved the death of his spiritual advisor, who had counseled and inspired him for more than twenty years.

No one is immune to grief. It's the great equalizer. All of us, whether rich or poor, intelligent or simple, successful or struggling, will someday come face-to-face with grief. Some have been destroyed by their grief. Most make the journey through grief with a few scars on the heart and some tender spots in their souls. And the truly blessed find grief to be a time to draw closer to God and to live life more fully, more gratefully, and more blessed.

We should all feel free to grieve in our own way. Other people may criticize or make comments about the way we are grieving or how long we are grieving. But this is not a time to be concerned about what other people think or say. This is the tenderest of times for us. We simply need to follow our hearts.

No One Understands

The uniqueness of our grief often causes us to groan that no one understands us. Two parents may grieve entirely differently at the loss of their child. Siblings will each grieve differently at the loss of a parent. And spouses all over the world grieve in different ways when they lose their life partner.

Those closest to us probably do not know how we are feeling or what they can do for us. At some point, in complete frustration, we may hear someone say to us—or we may even say ourselves—"What's the purpose of this? Why all the tears? Why all the sadness? What do we hope to accomplish?" We cannot bring the person back with anger, sadness, regret, remorse, or listlessness. Yet even if we try to pick ourselves up and shake ourselves off, sometimes we still feel this useless burden of grief. What can it accomplish?

The purpose of grief may not be found in psychological studies or MRIs of the grieving brain. Rather, one of the primary purposes of the grieving process might be found in the ancient writings of Scripture, which tell us we have an innate longing for God.

> O God, you are my God—
>   it is you I seek!
> For you my body yearns;
>   for you my soul thirsts,
> In a land parched, lifeless,
>   and without water. (Psalm 63:2)

> My soul yearns and pines
>   for the courts of the LORD.
> My heart and flesh cry out
>   for the living God. (Psalm 84:3)

A great benefit of grief might be that it makes us more fully aware of this spiritual longing. When a very special person is gone from our lives, the only One who can really understand us is God. Grief throws us into the arms of our loving God.

Shortly after her beloved husband died, St. Elizabeth Ann Seton wrote of this deeper connection with God in a letter to a friend: "I cannot doubt the Mercy of God who by depriving me of my dearest tie on earth will certainly draw me nearer to him."[1] The *Catechism of the Catholic Church* tells us this is a closeness we all crave: "The desire for God is written in the human heart, because man is created by God and for God" (27). And the *United States Catholic Catechism for Adults* expands on this truth: "God has planted in every human heart the hunger and longing for the infinite, for nothing less than God."[2]

When life is going well, we may not be aware of this deep longing for God. When we are busy with many things, we may not feel this divine tugging at our hearts. But when someone we love has been taken from us, we hunger for love in a way we have never known before. It is then that God can truly touch our hearts as he has never been able to reach us before.

When we need strength and understanding beyond what our family and friends can provide, God is the only answer. When we feel a hole in our heart because someone we loved has been taken from us, we become more aware—consciously or unconsciously—of our need for God. Maybe that is one of the purposes of grief. Grief, on one level, could be an invitation from God to slow down and get to know him better.

When the apostles were grieving in the upper room because Jesus had been killed, the Lord appeared to them and turned their grief into rejoicing. But Thomas was not there, and so he continued to grieve and to doubt. One week later, Jesus appeared again, when Thomas was there. He said to Thomas, "Bring your hand and put it into my side, and do not be unbelieving, but believe" (John 20:27). In the same way, when we are grieving, God is inviting us to put our hand into his side and to learn to believe in him. For his love is greater than any other love, and it can sustain us through all pain and all grief.

Try This

Because your grief is unique, you may need to find someone very special to help you through this journey. One of the saints mentioned above might be a good spiritual companion for you at this critical point in your life. Maybe you need to seek out the companionship of a friend who has experienced a similar grief. A religiously focused support group might be helpful. In extreme cases, in which grief is crippling or leading to suicidal thoughts, you should seek the help of a certified grief counselor. Don't try to handle your grief alone.

Confused and Afraid

Dear Lord,
I did not expect grief to be like this.
I feel confused and afraid.
My emotions are a jumble of anger, sadness,
and frustration.
And no one seems to understand.
I don't know where to turn or what to do next.
Yet somehow, in the depths of my heart,
I think you may hold the answer to this pain,
just as you are now holding the soul of someone very dear
to me in your hand.
I'm not sure that I can trust you right now.
I'm not sure that I even want to talk to you.

But I don't know what else to do.
So I drop my grief at your door.
And I ask you, please, to show me the way out of
this darkness
and back into the light of your love.
Please send me an angel, a saint, or a friend
to guide me through this, because I feel so all alone.
I need you beside me, please, O Lord. Amen.

CHAPTER 2

In a Fog

"I'm going to miss her, but I'll be okay," Steve confidently repeated over and over to friends and family at the wake. He was sure his words were true. It was three years since they had first received news of his wife's cancer. It had been a roller-coaster ride of hope and frustration, anger and acceptance, tears and cherished memories. But now it was over, and he was ready to move on.

As Paula's disease had progressed, Steve had mastered the cooking, laundry, shopping, and cleaning chores she had once done. He had become used to coming home to an empty house during her long hospital stays. Now he was ready to get back to a normal routine.

But the morning after the funeral, Steve lay in bed staring at the ceiling. He couldn't think clearly. When he finally stumbled into the kitchen, he felt as if he were in a place he had never been before. He couldn't even remember where they kept the coffee. It was as if a thick fog had penetrated his home and his brain. Nothing seemed to make sense anymore. The man who had efficiently handled Paula's care, his job, and all the routine household responsibilities suddenly didn't know what to do next.

Confused and Disoriented

Most people are completely unprepared for the lethargy that can overwhelm us in the face of grief. It can seem that any motivation to take the next step is gone. Sleep may elude us, yet it's also all we want to do. Our emotions can be an unpredictable jumble of emptiness, sadness, and anger. We walk in a deep haze. Not only are our eyes misty from tears, but our minds are clouded.

This feeling of being confused, sluggish, or disoriented is often referred to as being in a fog. By its very definition, physical fog reduces visibility, and we can't see clearly. So too, in the fog of grief, we may not be able to see the way ahead. We may not be able to imagine what life will be like from now on. We may want to stay cocooned in our bed or our home, feeling even more disoriented when we venture outside.

C. S. Lewis, the scholar, novelist, and poet, vividly described the foggy feelings of grief. Lewis is best known for *The Chronicles of Narnia* and *The Screwtape Letters*, but his most emotional book is *A Grief Observed*. In it Lewis documents his own overwhelming grief when his beloved wife, Joy, died after only four years of marriage and a long battle with cancer. The book was so powerful that friends often suggested Lewis read it, unaware that he had written it and then published it under a pen name. It was only after Lewis' own death that publishers were allowed to identify him as the author.

Lewis, a man who wrote about human emotions all the time, was completely surprised by his own grief. He told of fear, restlessness, and the inability to enjoy anything at all. He described the common fog of grief: "There is a sort of invisible blanket between the world and me, . . . spread over everything a vague sense of wrongness, of something amiss."[3] He also said that he felt he didn't even know what he wanted. This is a common feeling for many of us who grieve. Possibly because the one thing we want most cannot be returned to us, we have no idea what we want at all. Lewis spoke of not wanting to be alone but also not wanting anyone to talk to him. He suggested it would be nice if people were in his house but talked to one another and not to him.

St. Elizabeth Ann Seton was another who wrote of the fog of grief. When her oldest daughter died of tuberculosis, Elizabeth, who by that time was known as Mother Seton, wrote, "For three months after Nina . . . was taken, I was so often expecting to lose my senses and my head was so disordered that unless for the daily duties always before me I did not know much of what I did or what I left undone."[4] Like Elizabeth, we might only make it through the fog of grief on autopilot.

God of the Mists

Being on autopilot, however, is not a good way to travel through fog. Science tells us that fog is simply a low-lying cloud or a thick mist. Yet by any name, fog can be disorienting. Thankfully, as people of faith, we do not have to navigate the fog alone. For our God is a God of the fog and mist. From the dawn of time, God has made himself known to humanity in fog, clouds, and mist.

When God was leading his people out of Egypt, he led them by a column of cloud and by fire:

The LORD preceded them, in the daytime by means of a column of cloud to show them the way, and at night by means of a column of fire to give them light. Thus they could travel both day and night. (Exodus 13:21)

It was God, present in the fog, who inspired the Israelites to move forward or to stay where they were for a while:

Whether the cloud lifted during the day or the night they would then break camp. Whether the cloud lingered over the tabernacle for two days or for a month or longer, the Israelites remained in camp and did not break camp; but when it lifted, they broke camp. (Numbers 9:21-22)

At Jesus' transfiguration, God spoke to a few chosen apostles from a bright, thick fog:

Behold, a bright cloud cast a shadow over them, then from the cloud came a voice that said, "This is my beloved Son, with whom I am well pleased; listen to him." When the disciples heard this, they fell prostrate and were very much afraid. But Jesus came and touched them, saying, "Rise, and do not be afraid." (Matthew 17:5-7)

And the Book of Revelation tells us that in the end, God will come to us, no longer in a cloud but sitting on it:

Then I looked and there was a white cloud, and sitting on the cloud one who looked like a son of man, with a gold crown on his head and a sharp sickle in his hand. (Revelation 14:14)

So when we feel the fog of grief clouding our mind and making it difficult for us to think clearly, let's not be afraid. Instead, let's know that God has truly come to visit us. He is settling down with us, to give us time to nestle up close to him and come to grips with our deep loss.

In the Book of Kings, we read that God can be in the darkest cloud:

When the priests left the holy place, the cloud filled the house of the LORD so that the priests could no longer minister because of the cloud, since the glory of the LORD had filled the house of the LORD. Then Solomon said, / "The LORD intends to dwell in the dark cloud." (1 Kings 8:10-12)

When this dark cloud fills our own souls, let's remember the words of the wise Solomon and know that God is with us. He intends to dwell with us during this dark time.

Being Safe

Knowing God is in the fog may not help the hazy feeling go away. But it can help us navigate through the darkest times of our grief. It's often difficult to predict when a fog will lift, yet every fog eventually does lift. The sun does shine again. But what do we do while the fog is thick? Four of the safety tips for driving through physical fog may be useful when considering personal fog:

1. **Slow down.** We should give ourselves permission to move carefully. We don't make quick moves or serious decisions when in a fog. We should ask God to guide us in any decision we must make. He is right there with us.

2. **Use low lights.** Anyone who has ever tried to flash a bright light into the fog knows it makes things worse. It's okay to say, "It's too bright. It's too noisy." Quiet and stillness might offer the most comfort right now. We mustn't let others force us into situations that feel blinding. Instead, we turn to the gentle light that is the Spirit. God is our guide during this time.

3. **Don't stop in the middle of the road.** A person who panics and stops in the middle of a foggy road runs the risk of getting hit. In the same way, while we are going through the deep mists of grief, it's important to keep moving. As tempting as it might be to lock the doors, take the phone off the hook, and stay in bed, stopping is a dangerous thing to do. We need to move forward, but slowly and carefully.

4. **Pick a dependable line to guide you.** Safety experts recommend we watch the white line on the side of the road, rather than the center line or the broken lines that divide the lanes. The

white line on the side is a solid line. In grief, the only dependable solid line is God. Other people may want to guide and advise us, but their knowledge of our heart is not solid. Only God knows every tear we shed, every pain we feel, and every hurt that stabs into our very being. While in the deep fog of grief, it's important to never take our eyes away from God.

Toward the end of his personal journal on grief, C. S. Lewis concluded, "I need Christ, not something that resembles Him."[5]

Try This

Get an electronic candle with a timer. These inexpensive little candles can be set to glow for the same four-hour period every day. Set your candle to go on at a time that is darkest for you. Maybe have it light up in the morning, when you are sitting down to pray. Or program it to go on right before you come home every night to a dark and empty house. Or let it flicker softly as you fall asleep each night. Let this candle remind you that God is always there. He is the gentle light that will lead you through the fog and mists of your grief.

Walking in a Fog

God above,
I feel as if I am trapped in a thick, dense fog.
The world around me is only a wispy shadow of what it once was.

Everything is muted. All seems quiet.
I'm scared to make a move, afraid I will trip and fall.
I'm afraid of what lurks ahead of me now.
I feel darkness clinging to me like a damp mist.
I know you, O Lord, are a God who walks in the mist,
a God who shows up in the dense cloud.
Please walk with me now.
I think I can make it through this fog if you will be there
with me.
Could you please be a small light in the distance,
guiding me to the end of this heaviness?
Could you be the solid line for me to follow as I simply
take one small step at a time,
believing that moving forward is better than
standing still?
Could you soon blow the mists away with your
mighty breath,
letting your sun shine upon me once again?
I place my hand in yours and ask you, please, to lead me
out of this gray and terrible mist. Amen.

CHAPTER 3

Healing Tears

Sara insisted that she wanted to speak at her grandmother's funeral. Her father tried to talk her out of it, warning her that she would cry. But Sara was confident that if she rehearsed the words enough, she would be able to say them without crying.

Sara was wrong. Halfway through the eulogy, the reality of what she was doing hit her. As she stood in front of the church full of people and looked at her grandmother's casket, she realized she'd never again see the lovely woman she had loved so much. Suddenly all the tears she had been holding back began to flow. She tried to get herself under control, but her eyes were so blurred that she couldn't read the words on the page. She simply sobbed.

She wasn't sure how long she stood there crying, but suddenly her dad was by her side, leading her back to her seat. She was mortified. She didn't know how she could face friends and family after such an embarrassing show of emotion. Yet after Mass, all those who gathered around her were hugging her and saying, "That was beautiful. You loved your grandmother so much." And surprisingly, she felt okay. She was no longer mortified; she was comforted.

Jesus Wept

One of the shortest but most frequently quoted verses in the Bible is "And Jesus wept" (John 11:35). These three simple words recount Our Lord's reaction as he approached the tomb of his dear friend Lazarus. If Jesus weeping over the loss of a friend is not enough to assure us our tears are good and blessed, then the next verse may offer us the comfort we need: "So the Jews said, 'See how he loved him'" (11:36).

Through Our Lord's own example, we see that even though we may be embarrassed or frustrated by our tears, others do not view them as a sign of weakness. They see them as a sign of our great love for the one who has passed.

Perhaps we are uncomfortable with tears because most of us, as children, were admonished, "Stop crying! Stop being a baby! Grow up." As a result, we may resist crying, afraid our tears will make others uncomfortable. And of course, children need to learn to give up their infantile tears, which can be self-centered, inappropriate, and manipulative. But the tears of grief are of an entirely different order.

People of all times and all cultures have been very accepting of tears of grief. These are not childish or selfish tears. They are perhaps the most complex of tears, often a mixture of deep sadness, anger, loneliness, and fear. But mostly they are tears of love. They are genuine expressions of our love for the one we have lost. We should never be ashamed of them.

Tears are also a very important part of our healing process. They help wash away our sadness, anxiety, and fear. Yet we often apologize for them, murmuring, "I'm sorry," in between the sobs. We're more likely to feel uncomfortable with our own crying if we have felt uncomfortable when others have cried in front of us. This can be especially true if we are experiencing deep, sobbing grief for the first time in our lives. We are often surprised by the intensity of our emotion. That doesn't make our emotion—or the tears that express it—wrong.

The Science of Tears

When we struggle with tears, it might help to know that all tears are not created equal. Our body manufactures three different kinds. The first kind, called basal tears, keeps our eyes moist at all times. If we don't have enough basal tears, we have to buy "artificial tears" at the drugstore. The second kind is reflex tears. Our body manufactures these when there is some kind of irritant in the eye. Both of these forms of tears are important to the good health of our eyes, and no one is uncomfortable with them. The third kind is emotional tears—these are the ones that can distress us.

Our body spontaneously releases emotional tears in response to strong emotion or pain. Sorrow, joy, anger, stress, or physical pain can cause these tears. Most of us have learned strategies to control them, yet we will find it impossible at times to control emotional tears. The more intense the emotion or the pain, the less chance we have of stopping the tears. That is, in fact, a good thing.

Scientists know quite a bit about emotional tears. The chemical makeup of these tears is different from the chemical makeup of the first two kinds. Emotional tears contain stress hormones, endorphins, and other chemicals that can actually be soothing and numbing. So just as basal and reflex tears are good for our body, emotional tears can be chemically good for our emotional well-being. They literally can help us release overwhelming emotions that, if left trapped in the body, can lead to psychological and physical problems.

Researchers say that crying can be one of the best ways to naturally soothe ourselves. The longer we cry, the more chemicals we release. So having one good long cry can actually be better than constantly trying to hold back the tears. Research also shows that once we release these chemicals, we may experience a sense of calm or well-being. Apparently, in some part of ourselves, we still need to be like the baby who can cry uncontrollably, for a long stretch of time, and then suddenly roll over and fall into a deep, peaceful sleep.

It was these emotional tears that Our Lord wept. God cherishes this kind of tears. In Scripture, the psalmist thanks God for his compassionate care for our tears:

> Are my tears not stored in your flask,
> recorded in your book? (Psalm 56:9)

What a lovely, calming image: an angel silently gathers our tears, letting them flow into a special bottle with our name on it, and then whisks them away to heaven. There God, with tears in his own eyes, writes in his great book the day and the time we are crying.

A Time to Weep

The Bible offers another soothing and memorable verse about crying. It can be found in the popular poem about the right time for everything under the heavens. There is

a time to weep, and a time to laugh;
a time to mourn, and a time to dance. (Ecclesiastes 3:4)

While God tells us, through his word, that it is okay to cry for a while, he also tells us we must eventually set aside our crying and mourning. The only way to be ready for the laughing and the dancing, however, is to get all the tears out.

After Joyce's husband died, her daughters became upset with her because she insisted on setting a place for her husband at every major family gathering. They pointed out that it made her cry every time she set the plate and glass at his usual place. They demanded to know how long she was going to keep this up. She replied that she would do it until it no longer made her cry. One benefit of having the dishes set at her husband's place was that it gave those who gathered around Joyce's table permission to talk about him. And the more they talked, the more they told good stories, and the more they began to laugh. Amazingly, within a few months, Joyce found herself smiling instead of crying when she set his place, and she realized her time to cry had passed.

Although we might like to cry in private, researchers have also found that when we cry around someone who will be supportive, we usually feel better afterwards than we do when we cry alone. I will never forget the comforting feel of my brother's arm around me as I sobbed immediately following my father's death. I doubt I would have felt the same comfort and healing if I had run off to a corner to cry alone.

Of course, excessive or constant crying is not good and can even hamper the healing process. We must be careful to keep our crying within a good and reasonable time frame. Keep in mind that we are more inclined to cry if we are tired. Thus, staying up all night crying can lead to a bad pattern of crying too much and too often. Scripture also tells us there is "a time to heal" (Ecclesiastes 3:3). We must be aware of whether our tears are leading us to healing or keeping us stuck in grief.

Despite our best efforts to accept and understand our tears, there will be times when crying will annoy us. St. Ephrem, one of the earliest Doctors of the Church, had some words to help. Ephrem is credited with introducing hymns into the public worship of the Church. This man, who dedicated his life to helping worshippers lift their voices in joy, also believed, "Until you have cried, you do not know God."[6] For all of their benefits and inconveniences, our tears can truly draw us closer to God.

Try This

Give yourself permission to cry. Instead of being afraid to cry, plan a time and place to embrace your tears.

I had been avoiding places where I used to take my dad, because I knew they would make me cry. One day I decided to go for one last ride with Dad. I started in front of his house, as if I were picking him up, and followed the route we drove when I used to take him shopping, to the bank, and to the doctor. I imagined him in the car with me one last time, and I told him how much I missed him. I drove slowly and let the tears flow. For me, it was a healing and treasured drive.

Wash Away My Grief

Dearest Jesus,
you know the pain of weeping,
but you were able to call your friend Lazarus from
the tomb.
As much as I might wish it, my loved one will not walk
back into my life.
So my tears flow.
They exhaust me.
They embarrass me.
But in some strange way, they also comfort me.
Please let my tears wash away my pain and grief.
Wipe them gently from my face.
Send an angel to gather them and store them in heaven,
where I will need them no more.
I know you tell me there is a time to cry.
And I know you are with me, comforting me, even as
I sob.
But please, Lord, let this crying soon stop.
Show me how to smile and laugh and sing again. Amen.

CHAPTER 4

In Communion

After his wife's death, David tried to get back to his regular routine as much as possible. On the first Sunday morning after the funeral, he got up and went to Mass, as he and Peggy had always done. He pretty much zoned out through most of the Mass. But as the priest left the altar to distribute Communion, the organist and choir broke into the familiar notes of "On Eagle's Wings." And David lost it. He lost every bit of control he had been struggling to maintain for a week. "On Eagle's Wings" was one of Peggy's favorites, and it was the song they had sung as he and his family followed her casket out of church just five days before.

Biting hard on the inside of his lip to keep back the sobs, David rushed out of church, across the parking lot, and into his car. There he collapsed over the steering wheel and cried the gut-wrenching sobs he had been holding back for days. As quickly as he could, he pulled himself together and drove out of the parking lot before anyone saw him. Driving home, he vowed he would never go back.

The Real Presence

Elizabeth Ann Seton was the first native-born citizen of the United States to be canonized by the Catholic Church. Born in 1774 into an Episcopalian family in New York City, she married William Seton, a wealthy businessman, and together they had five children. But William contracted tuberculosis, and so, on the advice of doctors, the couple traveled to Italy, where it was hoped the mild climate would help William heal. Unfortunately, the trip didn't improve his health, but it did introduce Elizabeth to the Catholic faith of the friends with whom they were staying.

After the death of her husband, Elizabeth began to long for Jesus physically present in the Eucharist. She knew that the bread and wine were not merely symbols—they were the Body and Blood of Christ—and she felt that this Real Presence would soothe and heal her. On her return to New York, she would position herself in her Episcopal church so that she could look out the window at the Catholic church across the street. In this way, she would pray to Jesus in the Blessed Sacrament. Despite scorn and rejection from family and friends, Elizabeth eventually converted to Catholicism.

Elizabeth's longing to be in communion with Jesus is something we too, in our own way, may experience in our grief. Even as we long for Christ, we might feel uncomfortable attending Mass with a parish community that overwhelms us with their pity or good intentions. Like Elizabeth Ann Seton, we might want to just peek through the window of church and not actually go inside.

Yet we need Jesus, because he is the great healer. In the Gospels, we often hear of people who made most unusual attempts to get to Jesus. Zacchaeus climbed a tree (see Luke 19:2-10). The paralyzed man was dropped through the roof (see Mark 2:3-4). We too may need to find a unique way to get to Jesus during our time of grief.

We might avoid seeking Jesus in the Eucharist if we feel that our grief makes us different from those around us. We might feel like the blind man who cannot see, the lame man who cannot walk, the leper who is unclean, or the woman who suffered from the same ailment for years. We might feel like the disciples afraid of the storm, Peter's mother-in-law lying in bed and unable to serve, or the young girl who is dead. Yet if we take a few minutes to read chapters 8 and 9 in Matthew's Gospel, we will see that Jesus cured every one of these people of their suffering. He can cure us too of the suffering our grief is causing.

The Eucharist is the great "unifier," inviting the rich and the poor, the young and the old, the sick and the well, the employed and the unemployed. Jesus hosted the doubting, the loyal, the scared, and the betrayer at the first Eucharist on the night before he died. He also invites and welcomes the grieving to this greatest of feasts.

Only Say the Word

In the midst of our grief, we may not be ready to accept invitations to any parties or feasts, even the feast of the Eucharist. But it's important to realize that if we are searching for Jesus in the midst of our sorrow, the surest place to find him is in the Eucharist.

Nearly two thousand years ago, two disciples were walking down a road feeling the same kind of disbelief, loneliness, and sadness we often feel when we are grieving. Scripture tells us they were downcast. These disciples had once followed Jesus. They had been his friends. But now Jesus had been brutally beaten and hung upon a cross to die. Surely there could be no worse death than that.

When Jesus came alongside these two on the road to Emmaus, they didn't recognize him. That happens when we grieve: we may not recognize when Our Lord is walking beside us. So Jesus began a simple conversation with them. He asked them what they were talking about. Jesus listened to their grief and shared insights with them from the Old Testament, yet still they did not realize that God was walking with them. But when they stopped to rest and asked him to join them, "it happened that, while he was with them at table, he took bread, said the blessing, broke it, and gave it to them. With that their eyes were opened and they recognized him, but he vanished from their sight" (Luke 24:30-31).

Much has changed in this world in the last two thousand years. Much has changed in our own lives since we have experienced the death of a very dear and important person. But one thing never changes: we can always find Jesus in the breaking of the Communion bread. In the midst of our grief, let us take time to contemplate that Jesus truly is there. What a great gift, what a wonderful miracle, this is for us.

Not only is Jesus waiting for us in the Eucharist, but he is also ready to heal us from the pain of our grief. The words we say during the Communion Rite remind us of that. The celebrant lifts up the consecrated host and says, "Behold the Lamb of God." And we respond, "Lord, I am not worthy that you should enter under my roof, but only say the word and my soul shall be healed." These words come directly from Scripture. They're the words of the centurion who believed Jesus could heal his servant without even going to his house to touch the man. The centurion told Jesus, "Lord, I am not worthy to have you enter under my roof; only say the word and my servant will be healed" (Matthew 8:8). Matthew tells us, "And at that very hour [his] servant was healed" (8:13).

Like the centurion, we too must believe that Jesus can offer us healing when we turn to him in the Eucharist.

The Perfect Place to Be

Like Elizabeth Ann Seton, St. Thérèse of Lisieux found relief from her grief in Communion. Thérèse was only four years old when her mother died. She grieved deeply, and when she made her First Communion a few years later, she wept. Those around her presumed she was crying because she missed her mother. She said that wasn't the case. "As if the absence of my mother could make me unhappy on the day of my First Communion. As all Heaven entered my soul when I received Jesus, my mother came to me as well."[7] Thérèse's tears were tears of joy.

Church is the perfect place to be when we are grieving. Many people find that more frequent Mass attendance is helpful in their healing. Mass can be comforting because we are surrounded by others who are also bringing some grief to the Lord. The simple fact that most Masses are offered for loved ones who have died attests to the healing power of this perfect kind of prayer.

Also, during the Eucharistic prayer, we hear special prayers for those who have died, prayers that can be particularly meaningful to those who are grieving. The deceased are always remembered with beautiful words:

- Grant them, O Lord, we pray, and all who sleep in Christ, a place of refreshment, light, and peace.[8]
- Remember also our brothers and sisters who have fallen asleep in the hope of the resurrection and all who have died in your mercy.[9]
- Remember also those who have died in the peace of your Christ and all the dead, whose faith you alone have known. To all of us, your children, grant, O merciful Father, that we may enter into a heavenly inheritance with the blessed Virgin Mary, Mother of God, and with your Apostles and Saints in your kingdom.[10]

Thus, at every Mass we pray for our loved ones who have gone before us. As much as we might want to be alone in our grief, God calls us to be with others. When God first made us, he clearly stated, "It is not good for the man to be alone" (Genesis 2:18). And Jesus promised us, "Where two or three are gathered together in my name, there am I in the midst of them" (Matthew 18:20).

Many things are better when they are done in community. Watching a sporting event, taking a class, listening to music, and dancing are just a few activities that are better when we share them with others. Communing with God can also be more uplifting when done with other people.

In his apostolic exhortation The Joy of the Gospel, Pope Francis tells us what a great gift the Mass and Communion can be:

> The Eucharist, although it is the fullness of sacramental life, is not a prize for the perfect but a powerful medicine and nourishment for the weak.[11]

> To those who feel far from God and the Church, to all those who are fearful or indifferent, I would like to say this: the Lord, with great respect and love, is also calling you to be a part of his people![12]

Jesus is our power and our strength. When we are disconnected from him, we are like a light that is unplugged. We are unable to glow, no matter how many times we flick the switch or change the bulb. We simply need to be plugged back in.

Try This

If going to the same Mass you attended with your loved one is painful, consider a new option. Try going to Mass at a different time, at a different parish, or even at a local Catholic hospital, nursing home, or convent chapel. It may also help to attend a weekday Mass. These Masses are often quieter and have fewer distractions. They can allow you to connect with our Savior on a more personal level while you work up the strength to return to your regular Sunday Mass routine. Eucharistic Adoration is another way to be alone with Jesus. Check your diocesan website to find Mass times for other parishes and the closest Eucharistic Adoration chapel.

Longing for the Eucharist

Dear Lord, I long to be close to you.
I need to kneel in your presence.
I need to feel your loving embrace.
I need to look up and see you in the Eucharist.
I need to have your precious Body placed gently in
my hands.
But, God, I am afraid to enter your house.
I know you are there waiting for me.
Yet I am anxious.
I hesitate.
I make excuses.
I'm overwhelmed by memories.
I'm afraid of my unpredictable and
uncontrollable emotions.
Please, Lord, help me come to you in total trust
and confidence.
Let nothing keep me from you, O Lord.
Let nothing keep me from you.
When I'm fearful and want to turn away,
remind me that you are the Lamb of God

who can take away my pain and suffering.
Remind me that I'm blessed to be called to your Supper.
Remind me that through you I can be healed.
Thank you for that. Amen.

CHAPTER 5

Anger and Questions

Absolutely nothing was right about Kim's death. She was too young—only seventeen. She never should have been there. She was supposed to be home studying. But friends had talked her into sneaking out while her parents were at a neighbor's house watching the game. The man who hit their car had been drinking way too much. And the police didn't even contact Kim's parents until after she had died. The wave after wave of terrible wrongs left Kim's parents angry beyond belief. They were mad at everyone—including themselves and their friends, Kim's friends, the drunk driver, the police, and the emergency room workers.

But most of all, they were mad at God. Surely God could have prevented this. If only one little thing had gone right that evening, they would not be mourning the loss of their beautiful daughter.

Shocked beyond Belief

Whether tragic, sudden, or expected, death always seems to leave us with at least some anger and questions. We might think we are prepared for death. We might think our hand is firmly in God's and that we can handle anything with him by our side. But when death actually comes calling, it can leave us in a state of shock. We are not fully prepared for the reality of a cold, lifeless body, an empty house, memories that choke us with grief, and responsibilities we never faced before.

The shock of death can leave us acting in shocking ways. We may find ourselves being angrier, more emotional, more withdrawn, more confused, or more demanding than we ever thought we could be. The person who is reacting to this death may not be the person we always thought we were. When death leaves us shocked, we may find it helpful to take time to identify and accept all that is going on in our lives and in our minds. It's only when we recognize and accept our uncharacteristic behaviors that we can address them in helpful, healing, and holy ways.

It might be good to consider these two questions:

1. **What am I really feeling?** Our common reaction to grief might be anger or sadness, but when we dig a little deeper, we may discover a host of other emotions at play. These might be denial, guilt, envy, fear, loneliness, confusion, resentment, frustration, stupor, anxiety, bitterness, hopelessness, abandonment, or distrust. When we properly identify our emotions, we may realize that anger is not our biggest problem.

2. **Who or what is causing me to feel this way?** Once we have identified all the emotions our poor soul is trying to process as a result of the shock, we can start to look at who or what may be causing these emotions. We may discover that while all these emotions are natural, we may be directing them at the wrong people. For example, we may be blaming a nurse when the real cause of death was a lifetime of bad health choices.

Looking honestly and thoughtfully at our emotions can help us overcome them and heal. But often the most shocking realization may be that we are angry at God.

Angry at God

We may feel horrified to realize we are angry at God. Instead of uttering devout prayers, we may feel like shouting and yelling at him, "Answer me, Lord! Why did you let this happen? I no longer believe in you."

When these shocking prayers enter our minds, the first thing we should realize is that they are not wrong. It's better to rant and rave at God than to transfer our anger to people who may be trying to help us. We can shout to God things we may not feel comfortable whispering to even our closest friend. God understands our anger. God can handle it. More importantly, God—and God alone—can lovingly heal it.

We do not have to be afraid to express ourselves to God. Remember, God always knows what's in our hearts, whether we say the words or not. So we might as well talk to him about all the pain, the questions, and the anger. No one can deal better with these most tender and raw feelings than God. Scripture tells us it's okay to be angry: "Be angry but do not sin; do not let the sun set on your anger" (Ephesians 4:26). Anger itself is not a sin. However, we must not let our anger cause us to act in unkind or alienating ways with others. It's better if we lay that anger at the feet of God as soon as possible.

In his 2018 apostolic exhortation On the Call to Holiness in Today's World, Pope Francis encourages us to always turn to God when life is just too much for us: "When we feel overwhelmed, we can always cling to the anchor of prayer, which puts us back in God's hands and the source of our peace."[13]

Even Jesus got angry. In fact, it might be said that he had a bit of a temper tantrum when he threw the money changers out of the Temple. "He overturned the tables of the money changers and the seats of those who were selling doves" (Matthew 21:12). In our grief, we too may sometimes feel like throwing something.

And when Our Lord was dying on the cross, he cried out to God in seeming despair, "My God, my God, why have you forsaken me?" (Matthew 27:46). These were not Our Lord's own words; they are from Psalm 22. Generations of Jewish people had used them to cry out to God in anger and pain.

The good news is that this lament against God doesn't end in despair. Rather, it ends with reconciliation. The psalm leads us to see that God is indeed in his heavens, and he cares for all our pain. Trust in God is restored simply by crying out and knowing God is there. The psalm concludes:

And I will live for the LORD;
    my descendants will serve you.
The generations to come will be told of the Lord,
    that they may proclaim to a people yet unborn
      the deliverance you have brought. (Psalm 22:31-32)

The Painful Question

Depending on the circumstances of our loved one's death, the most painful question that may linger even after we have shouted out all our anger is simply "Why?" In particular, a death that is sudden or a death that comes after thousands of prayers for healing can leave us standing before God with our hearts in our hands, wondering if he even cares, if he even exists.

When we have questions, it's good to take them to God. After all, questions are a great way to start any conversation, and because prayer is simply conversation with God, questions can be a way to pray. We learn this through the Book of Job. We take this amazing book of the Old Testament for granted, but in his book *Everlasting Man,* G. K. Chesterton, a convert to Catholicism, reminds us how special Job's story is.[14] In a time when most people of the world thought of their gods as vengeful creatures who would curse and punish anyone who challenged them, Job showed us it was okay to question God. Job was a good and faithful man who lost his wife, his children, his home, and his livelihood. He didn't hesitate to raise his questions and his despair to God. And yet, Scripture tells us, "In all this Job did not sin, nor did he charge God with wrong" (Job 1:22).

I will give myself up to complaint;
   I will speak from the bitterness of my soul.
I will say to God: . . .
   Let me know why you oppose me.
   Is it a pleasure for you to oppress? . . .

Your hands have formed me and fashioned me;
    will you then turn and destroy me? . . .
You renew your attack upon me
    and multiply your harassment of me;
      in waves your troops come against me.
Why then did you bring me forth from the womb?
    I should have died and no eye have seen me. . . .
    I should have been taken from the womb to the grave.
(Job 10:1-3, 8, 17-18, 19)

Rather than punishing Job for daring to raise these questions, God replies with some of the most beautiful and powerful words in Scripture.

Where were you when I founded the earth?
    Tell me, if you have understanding.
Who determined its size? Surely you know? . . .
Have you ever in your lifetime commanded the morning
    and shown the dawn its place . . . ?
Have you entered into the sources of the sea,
    or walked about on the bottom of the deep? . . .
    Tell me, if you know it all.
What is the way to the dwelling of light,
    and darkness—where is its place?
(Job 38:4-5, 12, 16, 18-19)

This poetic description of God's awesome power and all that he has created for humanity continues for over seventy verses. At the end of God's discourse, Job realizes that God is the only One who has the power to ease his sorrow. His angry words turn to words of total trust:

> I know that you can do all things,
>   and that no purpose of yours can be hindered. . . .
> I have spoken but did not understand;
>   things too marvelous for me, which I did not know. . . .
> By hearsay I had heard of you,
>   but now my eye has seen you.
> Therefore I disown what I have said,
>   and repent in dust and ashes. (Job 42:2, 3, 5-6)

Chesterton points out that although God lovingly accepted Job's complaining, he didn't answer Job's questions. That's the truth of our relationship with God: he understands all, and we never will.

Only God sees the big picture. He may not answer our questions directly, but he will lead us to be more trusting of him, more at peace, more accepting of our situation and of other people. When we ask the questions and voice our anger, we open ourselves to receiving these benefits. It's well worth it.

Try This

A good way to defuse anger, regret, or worry is with a pen and paper. When you keep thoughts in your mind, they tend to be circular—the same things keep going around and around in your head. When you begin to write down what is bothering you, however, your thoughts will begin to flow. It's as if the pen releases a dam that has been letting pain build up inside you. You can write in a journal or write a letter. You can address your letter to God, to a living person, or even to the one who has died.

Pour out all your thoughts and emotions. You can save your writings, or you can destroy them as a symbolic way to rid yourself of your pain. Make sure you don't actually send angry letters that you may someday regret! The writing is meant to heal you, not hurt someone else.

Why, O God?

Heavenly Father,
I'm so angry, I don't know what to say.
Over and over again, I wonder why.
Night and day, I am haunted by painful memories.
I worry about what I might have done wrong.
I cry over things that cannot be changed.
All I want is answers.
I think answers would help.
But when I cry out to you, I get no answers.
I ask you, O Lord, who knows all and controls all,
Why now?
Why this way?
Please whisper in my heart some words that will give
me comfort.

Take away my anger and my questions.

Give me instead a growing peace and trust in you.

Help me realize I do not need to know the answers or redo the past.

I just need to rest in your loving embrace.

Help me, please, O Lord, to do only that.

Comfort me, O Lord! Amen.

CHAPTER 6

Help!

It seemed Betty had not stopped crying since her mother died. She missed her so much. She'd been a wonderful mother who had lived a good life well into her nineties. She'd only been sick in the last year, and during that time, Betty tenderly cared for her. Now she was gone.

Her mother had been a woman of faith, ready to go to her eternal reward, but Betty wasn't ready to let her go. She felt like an abandoned orphan, overwhelmed by her grief. With each bout of tears, Betty felt more alone. Today was one of her bad days. Dropping to her knees, she prayed over and over, through the tears, the only prayer she could think of, "Lord, please help me."

Exhausted from her tears, she tried to distract herself with routine household chores, but a knock at the front door interrupted her. A neighbor stood there. "I hope I'm not intruding, but I lost my mom last year. I know how hard it can be. I just wanted to see if there was anything I could do." "Oh, my gosh," Betty exclaimed. "You're not intruding. You're a gift from God!"

The Source of All Help

Grief can truly be one of the most painful, stressful, and confusing experiences of our lives. Often we don't know where to turn for help. Because we all handle grief differently at different times in our lives, friends and loved ones may not understand what our unique needs are for the particular grief we are experiencing. We can't go to the pharmacy and pick up a package of "GriefAid." And we can't search for a good "grief doctor" online or in the yellow pages. Although a grief counselor may be helpful in cases of severe, disabling grief, many people feel there is a stigma in using professional help. So where do we go for the very special kind of help we need? The answer is simple. We go to God.

In his book *The Imitation of Christ*—considered one of the greatest spiritual guides of all time—Thomas à Kempis described perfectly why we must turn to God in our grief. He prayed, "Send me your help, Lord, in time of trouble, for help other than yours is no help at all."[15] Quite simply, people may fail us, but God never will.

We may feel we are unworthy of God's wonderful consolation. We may ask, as Thomas à Kempis did, "What have I done, Lord, that you should console me from heaven?"[16] The simple fact is that none of us can ever be worthy of God's grace and mercy. Yet he is always ready to offer us comfort and healing.

God assures us throughout Scripture that he is by our side night and day, even when no one else seems to be there. The psalmist knew it.

> I raise my eyes toward the mountains.
>> From whence shall come my help?
> My help comes from the LORD,
>> the maker of heaven and earth.

He will not allow your foot to slip;
   or your guardian to sleep.
Behold, the guardian of Israel
   never slumbers nor sleeps. (Psalm 121:1-4)

God assured the prophet Jeremiah of the same thing: "When you call me, and come and pray to me, I will listen to you" (29:12). And Jesus assures us that he is there for us: "Ask and it will be given to you; seek and you will find; knock and the door will be opened to you" (Matthew 7:7).

Our closest friends or family may not understand our grief, but God can provide help from the most unexpected places and in the most surprising ways. We need to be willing to cry out our plea and then open our hearts to the miracles he may send.

The Grace of Humility

When God sends help to our door, our response may be "I'm doing okay. I don't need anything." We may feel like being left alone. If we are going to heal from our grief, however, we usually need someone to help us. Despite what we may have learned as we grew up and became responsible adults, we don't always have to be strong and self-sufficient. Sometimes we need to be weak so that we can learn how amazingly strong and wonderful God is. When we are strong, we leave little room for God. But when we are weak—ah, that is when miracles can happen!

St. Teresa of Avila once said that true humility is "to know what [you] can do and what God can do."[17] When we face grief, we need the humility to admit that it will take God, working through other people, to get us through it. Pope St. John XXIII believed, "When we are humble, God comes to our aid." But he also lamented, "If only I knew how to be humble!"[18]

Sadly, in today's world, few of us are very humble. We must pray not only for help but also for the grace of humility, so we can graciously accept the help we need. Admitting we cannot do it alone allows some other person to be the hands and feet of Jesus for us.

When we accept help, we can establish new friendships or deepen the relationships we already have. People who offer help want to show, in some tangible way, that they care. We are giving them a gift by accepting what they offer. We allow them to show compassion and love.

However, we still have the right to remain in control. Humility doesn't mean that we allow others to bully us into doing things we're not ready to do, such as changing residences, giving away possessions, or becoming dependent on others to do things we should do ourselves.

It's best for us to work *together* with those who come to help. We'll regret it if we sit alone in our grief and let others do the work around us. If we wallow in the belief that we can no longer do anything, our normal grief can become a permanent and crippling condition. We might need help with new tasks while our grief is intense, but our goal must be to eventually heal the grief and resume normal activities. We don't want to live in grief forever.

Being in desperate need of help is a humbling experience. It's also a gift from God. It helps us realize, as never before, that we are a member of the body of Christ and just a member—not the whole body, not the head, not the heart, and not the brain. Just a little bit of flesh. And we need the flesh and blood of others to help us. Once we come to that realization, we are ready to receive help gratefully rather than begrudgingly. For many of us, being at the end of our rope helps us understand how important compassion can be. As we accept the compassion of others, we also learn how to give compassion. When we know what it feels like to need help, we become much better at giving help.

There is a woman who brings a large bag of food for the poor to our parish every week. When I commented once on her amazing generosity, she said she had been hungry as a child. She knew what hunger felt like. In the same way, we may someday help someone in their time of grief because now we know what grief feels like.

Resisting Loneliness

Even if we don't need physical help with tackling new chores or cleaning up the pieces left by death, we still need people to journey with us through our grief. Loneliness is a terrible thing. We may be lonely because an important person in our life is no longer there. Or we may feel lonely and isolated because we don't know what to say to others about our grief, and they don't know what to say to us.

Although it's tempting to retreat into loneliness, we need others in our life at this most tender time. We might be able to grieve alone, but we won't get over it alone. Needing someone isn't a sign of weakness. And we can take the initiative; we don't have to sit around and wait for someone to reach out to us. Most people will be happy to hear from us. People want to help, but they don't know if they will be imposing. As one woman said about spending time with a grieving friend, "I have no idea what she is going through, and I will not pretend that I do, but I will listen." We must find someone who will listen to us. This might be the biggest help we can use right now.

Getting over the social awkwardness that comes with grief is critical. We all have a need to "belong." Human beings are social animals; living lonely is not a good choice and can actually be harmful to our health. Studies have shown that those who are lonely are often more prone to disease, regardless of their age or physical condition before they became isolated. We must look to others to help us avoid painful loneliness.

The more we collapse in on ourselves, the lonelier we are going to be. And social media may not help. In fact, for many grieving people, social media can actually be more alienating than fulfilling. Conversation on social media is often one-sided, somewhat self-centered, shallow, and boastful. It's not necessarily healing or helpful. It doesn't foster close relationships. We need someone to hold our hand, not a device to hold in our hands. We might want to avoid social media if we find it painful during our grieving.

Even if we turn off Facebook and whatever connection we may find there, we shouldn't avoid personal interaction in real life. If being around people we know is painful right now, we might join a grief support group. Or we could get involved in an activity in which we can meet new people who will not identify us by our loss. Volunteering, joining a book club, taking a class, and being part of a Bible study group are a few ways to reach out to others who can help us in our healing, even if they don't know or understand our loss. They help us go on. And that is what we need to do.

Try This

Make a list of what you need. Grieving people often find lists helpful in getting their lives back into some kind of order. Pray over the list. Ask God to help you see what you need to do and who you need to help you. Where the answers are clear, reach out, and ask for the help you need. Where the answers are not clear, lift up your concerns to God in prayer. Believe that he will send you the people and the resources you need in the most unexpected ways. And then watch to see God at work.

Being Humble

Dear Lord,
I need help.
This is painful for me to admit.
I often take pride in being able to take care of
things myself.
But this great loss, this terrible sadness, I cannot
handle alone.
I know you are with me, but I need others to physically
walk with me on this journey.
Please send me the people I need.
Show me how to be humble and gracious in accepting
help from family, friends, and strangers.
Teach me, through my present need,
how to someday be caring and helpful to someone else.
Let me welcome and appreciate the help you send.
Please give me the grace to see you in those who come to
my aid.
Wash away my pride and loneliness.
Let me be humble.
I trust in you, O great Lord. Amen.

CHAPTER 7

Images of God

Cindy sat alone, sobbing at the side of her husband's bed. The nurses who had been there during the final moments had discreetly stepped away, leaving her with her heartbreak and disbelief. It all seemed so impossible. He was too young. They should still have many years ahead of them. It had been too fast, too sudden. All the doctors, the painful chemo, and the ridiculously expensive medications were supposed to stop this. She was aware of people gently coming in and out of the room, but she refused to acknowledge them.

Some part of her insanely thought that if she did not get up from this chair, if she did not let go of her husband's cold hand, she would awake, and this would all be a terrible nightmare. But now she felt someone standing next to her—a religious sister. "Would you like me to pray with you?" the sister softly asked.

"I don't want to talk to a God who would do this to me," Cindy angrily answered.

Sister placed a small crucifix on the bed next to Cindy's hand. "Can you maybe talk to a God who would do this for you?"

Who Is God to Us?

It will be difficult for us to turn to God in our sorrow if we have negative images of him. If we had a stern or abusive father, it might be hard to imagine God as a loving Father. If we were taught as children that God was watching and waiting for us to do wrong, we may want to avoid this judging God.

These kinds of negative images will not help us heal. We need a God who is kind and compassionate. Fortunately, that is exactly the God we have. The negative childhood images are wrong. The truth is that God, quite simply, is love.

Thankfully, Scripture is full of stories of this loving God. We should take time to consider which ones speak to us in our grief. The practice of drawing closer to God by placing ourselves with him in a scene from Scripture is an ancient tradition that many saints have endorsed. It's based on the idea that, because Scripture is the living word of God, it's good for us to imagine ourselves actually being in that word or that story. When he was a young man in the seminary, Pope St. John XXIII wrote a rule for himself: "When I am praying and at all other times, I will imagine myself in the presence of Jesus and with him on some occasion of his life."[19] This is definitely a good way for us to connect with Our Lord in the midst of our grief.

Many find relief from grief by thinking of Jesus as the Good Shepherd who will gently seek us out in our time of distress, pick us up, and carry us to safety. We can find comfort in a God to whom we can pray,

> Even though I walk through the valley of the shadow of death,
>> I will fear no evil, for you are with me;
>> your rod and your staff comfort me. (Psalm 23:4)

St. Thérèse of Lisieux liked the image of Jesus sleeping in her boat, as he was asleep in the apostles' boat when a storm blew (see Matthew 8:23-27). Can it bring us comfort to picture

Jesus asleep in our boat as we float down the river of grief? Do we need to nudge him in the middle of the night and ask, "Are you awake?" If we do, he will answer, "Yes, I am awake. I have not slept in forever."

We might like the image of Jesus crying at the tomb of Lazarus. Is Our Lord crying because of the death of his friend Lazarus or because of the sorrow he sees in his friends Martha and Mary? Either way, the image of a crying Jesus wrapping his arms around us at the grave of our loved one might be one we want to hold in our hearts.

The "Holy Three in One"

As we consider the many loving images of God found in Scripture, we might not be able to pick just one to comfort us. That's okay because we have a Triune God, three unique and different persons all in one God. This unity among God the Father, God the Son, and God the Holy Spirit is sometimes referred to as the "Holy Three in One." A different Person of the Trinity might be most healing for us at different times on our grief journey.

When I was a little girl, I thought my dad could fix anything—even popped balloons! He perpetuated this belief by keeping a bag of balloons hidden on his workbench. When my balloon popped, I would run to him, and he would blow up a new balloon for me. Fixed! I believe that our heavenly Father wants to fix things for us too, just as so many good fathers here on earth want to do. Granted, God the Father may not have a bag of balloons on his workbench, but he is the One to help us through what may be broken in our lives. He is the ultimate Father who can fix anything because he is the great Creator who made it all. He is the One who holds the world in his hands.

The Father is not a God to fear but a God to love. This is the God we can run to when we are hurt and crying. He can wipe away our tears and our pain. He is a God of extreme tenderness and mercy. Jesus introduced us to this God by telling the story of a father who waited every day for his son's return (see Luke 15:11-32). God the Father is always waiting to welcome each of us with joy, gentleness, and generosity. Even if we have not been close to this God before, now is a time to run to him and fall at his feet. He will embrace us with loving arms and lift us up out of our misery.

If we need someone who understands our pain, then God the Son is the One who can help. This is the God who knew human suffering. This is the God we see slumped over a large stone in the Garden of Gethsemane, torn with despair, fear, and suffering. This is who I personally like to turn to when I am hurting. I imagine myself creeping up next to him in the garden while the apostles are asleep. He reaches out with one hand and wraps his cloak around me, and together we cry upon the rock. I whisper over and over again, "I am sorry," and he smiles and says, "It will be okay. This too shall pass."

Christ crucified shows us a God who will do anything for us. The risen Jesus, who walks through a locked door to show the apostles his glorious wounds, is a God who reminds us that he will conquer death for all of us and unite us again in heaven (see John 20:19, 20).

When we need God to guide us out of the darkness and help us know what our next step should be, we can pray to God the Holy Spirit. This is the Person of the Trinity who brings us great gifts. The gifts of the Holy Spirit include wisdom, understanding, knowledge, fortitude, and awe. Who among us does not need at least one of these gifts as we journey through grief? The Spirit's gifts—when we accept them—bring wonderful fruits, such as patience, gentleness, self-control, peace, and joy.

The Holy Spirit has often been described as a wind, fire, breath, water, and a dove. We might imagine the Spirit with us when we feel a gentle breeze on our face. We can connect with this Spirit by taking deep breaths and praying, "Come," as we inhale and "Holy Spirit," as we exhale. In Italy, by tradition, churches rain down red rose petals on the congregation on Pentecost. The rose petals look like tongues of fire. A red rose, with its lovely scent and symbolism of love, might also be a way to connect us with this great Spirit.

God in Nature

If our sadness is so overwhelming that we have difficulty relating to the God found in Scripture, we may want to step outside. We can always find God in nature. The vastness of the skies shows us his awesome power. The minute details of an insect or a flower show us his tender care.

During the time that she grieved the death of her mother, the young Thérèse of Lisieux found comfort in nature. In her autobiography, *The Story of a Soul,* she tells of once being awed by a thunderstorm:

> Far away there was the rumble of thunder and flashes of lightning. I looked all around, not wanting to miss any of this awe-inspiring sight and was not the slightest bit frightened but quite delighted when I saw a thunderbolt fall in a nearby meadow. God seemed very near.[20]

Elizabeth Ann Seton too found comfort from her grief in the beauty of nature. She was only three when her mother died. She quickly learned that she could soothe her loss by looking up into the heavens. It was there that she imagined her mother to be, and it was in the beauty of the sky that she also came to know God as the awesome Creator of all that was beautiful. Again, when her beloved husband, William, died, she looked to the sky for peace and hope. She found the power and beauty of God in the sunsets and the dawn.

Nature is a beautiful and natural place to find God. We can feel him in a glorious sunset, a quiet trail, a bubbling brook, or a mountain view. We may look at a small statue and think this God is not big enough to care for our great pain. But when we look at the vastness of the universe or the intricacy of a butterfly's wings, then we know that God is more than big enough to care for every whisper and every tear in every heart.

Try This

Take time to be completely alone with God. Sit in a quiet and comforting place. Imagine who God is to you. Feel him with you. Let him touch your heart. Talk to him in your own words.

Or get out and take a walk with God. Look for him in the beauty around you. Put your hand on the trunk of a tree, or bend down to lay your hand flat on the earth. Feel the heartbeat of God in all he has created.

Look for a rock that catches your eye. Pick it up as a gift from God. Scripture often refers to God as our rock. Keep the rock in your pocket to remind you of the solid strength of God through your most difficult times.

I Need You, God

Awesome God,
I'm looking for you to comfort me in this grief.
But I'm not sure where to find you.
Please do not hide from me in this sorrowful time of my life.
I need to know you better than I have known you in the past.
I need to feel you as I have never felt you before.
Lead me to the places where I can find you.
Guide my hands as I page through my Bible.
Guide my eyes as I search for you in the heavens.

Guide my steps as I wander through my day looking for you.

Guide my heart as I open it to you—Father, Son, and Holy Spirit.

Let me find you, dear God.

Let me feel you near.

Let me hear your whisper in my soul.

For you alone can heal my grief.

I very much need you beside me now.

Thank you for always being there. Amen.

CHAPTER 8

Courage

When I walked into my Dad's hospital room after meeting with the hospice team, he was holding court. Family and friends were gathered around his bed as he shared his last bit of wisdom and stated his final instructions. "And you," he said pointing his finger at me as I came to stand at the end of the bed, "you be strong."

"I am strong, Dad," I assured him. "I just signed twenty-four papers for you."

The papers were necessary to transfer him to hospice. Although it had been Dad's decision, I was the one who had to sign for him. Little did I know that those would be the last intelligible words my dad would speak to me.

Within minutes nurses and paramedics were swarming around him. They began disconnecting him from some of the machines and meds that had kept him alive for the last ten days. He was transferred to the hospice facility from which—without all the advanced medical assistance—he would be gone in less than twenty-four hours. Dad's words, "You be strong," and the prayers of many wonderful people carried me through a hurt I would never have been strong enough to handle on my own.

Being Strong

My dad's last words have been a great gift to me. Dad knew grief. He had lost both of his parents before he was thirty. He watched my mom slip away with Alzheimer's. After her death, he used to tell me, "It is hard to live with the ghosts." My dad knew I would need strength and courage to battle my own grief when he was gone.

Dad's words to me were not that much different from the words King David spoke on his deathbed to his son Solomon. The Old Testament tells us,

> When the time of David's death drew near, he gave these instructions to Solomon his son: "I am going the way of all the earth. Be strong and be a man! Keep the mandate of the LORD, your God, walking in his ways and keeping his statutes, commands, ordinances, and decrees as they are written in the law of Moses, that you may succeed in whatever you do, and wherever you turn." (1 Kings 2:1-3)

We all need King David's words of wisdom to make it through grief. Be strong, and walk in the ways of the Lord.

Healing from grief doesn't come easily. It can require hard work and courage. We may need courage to touch painful memories, deal with anger, or move forward. If our pain is severe, we may need the courage to seek professional help or spiritual counseling.

Anne Morrow Lindbergh, who dealt with the tragic and very public grief of having her infant son kidnapped and murdered, wrote,

It isn't for the moment you are stuck that you need courage, but for the long uphill climb back to sanity, faith, and security.[21]

Grief can't be shared. Everyone carries it alone. His own burden in his own way.[22]

Wish me courage and strength and a sense of humor. I will need them all.[23]

Fortunately, courage is available to us as a gift from the Holy Spirit. The Holy Spirit offers his gifts most fully when we are most in need of them. Thus he offers us courage at the time we are most tempted to be weak. All we have to do is ask for this gift.

St. Paul, in his letter to the Ephesians, gives us good advice for being strong:

Draw your strength from the Lord and from his mighty power. Put on the armor of God. . . . In all circumstances, hold faith as a shield. . . . And take the helmet of salvation and the sword of the Spirit, which is the word of God. (Ephesians 6:10-11, 16, 17)

Doing the Impossible

St. Paul's strong military language might seem extreme, but we actually do have to go to battle against grief. Grief makes us weaker than we may have ever been before. It tempts us to turn away from our faith, to become bitter, and to surrender to self-pity and negativity. We may feel that we are powerless to fight the sadness. Yet God will give us the strength and the courage we need.

Throughout all the grief and trials of her life, St. Elizabeth Ann Seton felt this. She firmly believed, "Jesus can never give you a task above your courage, strength or ability."[24] Even when it takes courage just to get out of bed, to walk into the office, to meet a friend for coffee, or to go to church on Sunday, we must believe that Jesus is there, giving us that courage.

At some point, we will need that divine courage to take back control of our lives. We must make a choice to jump into the river of our world and swim upstream against the current of grief. This river may seem too cold, too deep, or too scary. But we can do it, and we must do it. We must grab hold of our courage—the courage that is God beside us—and jump back into life.

We need to be brave enough to experience all of the negative emotions but also strong enough to move beyond them. It can be tempting to live in our sadness rather than fight to overcome it. Sometimes we are more comfortable locked away from the world than emerging as a new person who has lost a critical part of who we once were.

A popular military motto says, "The difficult we do at once; the impossible takes a little longer."[25] This can be good wisdom for our fight against our grief. It may seem that it will be impossible to get over our grief. Certainly it will not be easy. But if we take one difficult step each day, we will wake up one morning and realize we are moving slowly and surely back into a new and acceptable life. With God we can do the impossible. Jesus promised this in the Gospel of Matthew: "For human beings this is impossible, but for God all things are possible" (19:26). If we take God along for this journey through grief, we will find it possible to do the painful and difficult things we might think are impossible.

Letting God

The hardest part of the grief journey is not the beginning. The first days after a death can be a blur of activity that almost makes us forget what has happened. Then family and friends who supported us during the wake and funeral return to their normal routines. Suddenly we seem alone. This is where the hard part begins. Here is where we most need courage to admit our pain and work to overcome it. Without courage, we either become stuck, or we live in denial. Courage lets us admit the loss and gradually let it go.

Letting go of our physical need for the loved one in our life is actually a form of sacrifice. We can hold on to our precious memories, but we must let go of the one who is now in God's arms. We think of sacrifice as a terrible thing, but the word "sacrifice" means "to make holy." When a loved one dies, we are asked to sacrifice that loved one back to God. To lift our dearly departed up to God and say, "I am offering back to you the great gift that you gave to me" is a way to make our entire grief experience a holy experience.

Granted, we had no choice in the death, but we do have a choice in making it a holy sacrifice to God. It takes courage to let go in this way. It's the kind of courage Jesus had when he walked up Cavalry to sacrifice his life for us. Because Jesus had such amazing courage, he can show us how to have courage.

In the Gospels, Jesus often tells his followers to "take courage" or to "be not afraid." One example of this occurs in Matthew's story of Jesus walking on the water. During a storm at sea, the apostles think they see a ghost walking on the water. But Jesus calls out to them, "Take courage, it is I; do not be afraid" (Matthew 14:27).

The apostles were amazed to see Jesus doing the impossible. He was walking on water. Peter wanted to do the same, so Jesus called him to come across the water. Although Peter confidently climbed out of the boat, he took his eyes off Jesus and became afraid. He started to sink. This can happen to us too, if we take our eyes off God during our grief.

Some days we will feel that we can do the impossible; we can walk through our grief. But when we take our eyes off Jesus, we'll become afraid of a stormy new future. We'll start sinking. We'll want to climb back into our safe little boat of grief. But if God tells us to have courage, we must believe he will also give us that courage. Jesus assured us of this during the Last Supper: "In the world you will have trouble, but take courage, I have conquered the world" (John 16:33).

Try This

Courage can be an unpredictable and fleeting thing. You might feel brave one moment but then anxious the next. This is why words of encouragement are so important. Whether we are fans at a game urging on our team or mentors sharing advice, encouragement can make a crucial difference.

Because your grief journey will be a series of ups and downs, it might be helpful to hide words of encouragement for yourself. Consider tucking favorite Bible verses, words from sympathy cards, or motivating slogans into places where you will see them later. If you hide encouraging words in pockets, dresser drawers, coffee cups, or books, you may be surprised at how often God will have them pop back up just when you need them most.

A Prayer for Courage

Heavenly Father, this grief is so much harder than I thought it would be.
I don't think I have the strength for it.
I need your help.
Please give me the courage to face all the pain, confusion, and uncertainty
with the sure knowledge that you are beside me
—leading and guiding me every step of the way.
Let your Spirit shower the gift of courage upon me.
Give me strength for this terrible battle.

Help me accept this loss and move forward bravely
and confidently.

Help me do the right thing, even when it seems impossible f
or me to do anything.

May every difficult decision I make today be good and
pleasing to you.

Lead me forward when I'm tempted to retreat into my sorrow.

Let the light of your love guide me through this darkness.

When it's hard to look ahead, and it's painful to look back,
help me keep my eyes on you.

Hold me up as I lift my loved one up to you.

With tears in my eyes and pain in my heart,

I surrender to you the one who has returned to you.

Give me the strength to step into the future with only
treasured memories

and a firm commitment to accept the new life you have
planned for me.

I trust in you completely, dear God. Amen.

CHAPTER 9

At the Cross

The minute Eileen pulled into the driveway, she knew something was wrong. It was a beautiful Saturday afternoon in early spring. Her son should not be sitting alone on the front porch looking utterly miserable. He was a senior in high school. He was endlessly busy—never home. "What's wrong?" she asked, getting out of the car. In an instant, he was in her arms sobbing, "Rodney was killed last night."

Suddenly everything became unreal. As if watching from a distance, she heard herself keening—wailing in a primitive way that came from deep in her soul. Over and over again, she cried out, "No, no, no!" The sudden and tragic death of such a vibrant young man was completely unacceptable and unbelievable. Wave after wave of overwhelming grief hit her as she thought of all those whose lives were forever changed: the young man—gone too soon; his parents and family; her son and his friends; all the students and faculty at the school, where this popular boy's chair would be empty at graduation.

Some deaths are just too shocking and overwhelming for us to understand. They make no sense. They bring unbearable pain. We scream at the assault.

Surrender

When we encounter a grief that is too tragic or overwhelming, there is only one place for us to go. That is to the foot of the cross. There we see the most horrible and unfair death of all. There we see Our Lord's grief-stricken mother and friends. It's from this scene, more than any other, that we may possibly learn to survive our grief.

Think of Mary, the apostle John, the other women at the cross. How very confused, how very angry, how totally destroyed they must have felt. Their plans were ruined. They didn't expect Jesus to die, especially not in such an appalling way. They had no idea what was coming next. They were fearful. Nothing made sense anymore. Where would they go from here?

We, at the death of a loved one, may feel many of these same things. So what can we learn from those who were at the foot of the cross?

One thing to notice is that no one stood at the cross alone. Those who lost Jesus clung to one another. In his dying moments, Jesus asked Mary and John to redefine their lives—to become mother and son, son and mother, to each other. In the same way, we are called to surrender who we once were and to become someone new. But we are not asked to do it alone. Loneliness is too great a cross for us to bear.

The more horrible our grief, the more we will need others to stand with us. Our grief only becomes heavier when we throw self-pity on top of our cross. Becoming bitter and thinking no one else understands or carries a cross as heavy as ours will not help our healing.

We may feel anger towards a God who would give us such a terrible cross. But when we consider the crucifixion, we realize that God the Father, Jesus his Son, Mary, and St. John all have known suffering like ours. They can show us how to surrender to God's eternal plan. They can show us how to pick up the cross of our grief—no matter how heavy it may seem—and move forward, even if only one small step at a time. The more willing we are to carry this cross, the lighter it will eventually become for us. It will become a part of us that we carry with love and acceptance.

The Greatest Love

Another lesson we can learn from the cross is the importance love plays in our healing. When death takes away a great love from our lives, we must not give up on love. Rather, it's better for us to take comfort in the greatest love of all time—the love Our Lord showed for each of us when he allowed himself to be nailed to a cross.

St. John, who stood at the foot of that cross, could have been bitter. Even after Jesus had risen from the dead, John could have been angry with Jesus for making his friends endure such horror. Just as we may question why our loved ones had to suffer too much or die too soon, the apostles struggled to understand why Jesus had to suffer and die. Even today it's one of the mysteries of our faith. But John never wrote of bitterness. John never demanded answers. Instead, he stressed love in all his writings.

Possibly because he was a witness to the crucifixion, but certainly because he knew the ways of Jesus so well, he was able to write, "We have come to know and to believe in the love God has for us. / God is love, and whoever remains in love remains in God and God in him. . . . We love because he first loved us" (1 John 4:16, 19).

In writing his Gospel, John preserved for us Jesus' own words on love: "This is my commandment: love one another as I love you. No one has greater love than this, to lay down one's life for one's friends" (15:12-13).

Why is Our Lord's great love for us so important as we struggle to heal from grief? Perhaps Pope Francis said it best in Joy of the Gospel: "Whenever we take a step towards Jesus, we come to realize that he is already there, waiting for us with open arms."[26] The arms that wait for us are the same arms that were stretched out on a cross. These arms are part of Jesus' broken body, offered for our healing. These arms hold out powerfully healing hands.

When Jesus walked the earth, people knew the healing power of his great love. Scripture tells us, "Everyone in the crowd sought to touch him because power came forth from him and healed them all" (Luke 6:19). And we remember the woman who came up behind Jesus to touch the fringe of his cloak, believing, "If only I can touch his cloak, I shall be cured" (Matthew 9:21).

Touch is a key part of one of the most beautiful liturgical services of the year, the Veneration of the Cross on Good Friday. All around the world, believers come forward to touch, kiss, or embrace a cross, often a life-size one. They come wearing shoes or barefoot, hobbling with canes or in wheelchairs, alone or carrying small children. Some carry heavy burdens—illness, job loss, broken marriages, drug-addicted children, and grief. With just their touch, they unite their sorrow with Our Lord's. It's a most powerful prayer. We can be inspired by watching this procession of hurting people coming to the cross. But more importantly, we can be healed by joining the procession.

I Thirst

Last words can be precious. We may treasure last words from our loved one, or we may mourn the fact that we have no good last words. Scripture does tell us some of Our Lord's last words. Right before he died, "he said, 'It is finished.' And bowing his head, he handed over the spirit" (John 19:30). Immediately before that, St. John tells us, Our Lord said, "I thirst" (19:28). Spiritual writers throughout the ages have reflected on these words of Christ. They say that Jesus was not just crying out for water; he was crying out for us to offer him our love and devotion. He was crying out for us to see his suffering as a sign of his never-ending love and mercy for us.

For Mother Teresa, those words, "I thirst," inspired her ministry to the sick and dying of Calcutta. She believed God thirsted for a loving connection with each and every person. That was her ministry: to bring people to God in the midst of their greatest suffering and to bring God to them. At our time of grief, we too are thirsting for God, and God is thirsting for us.

Jesus promises to relieve our thirst. He told the Samaritan woman at the well, "Whoever drinks the water I shall give will never thirst; the water I shall give will become in him a spring of water welling up to eternal life" (John 4:14).

We may want to go back to being the person we were before grief, but God can do even more for us. Just as he did for the woman at the well, he can transform us with the spiritual waters of his love and grace. He can refresh us. As water gradually erodes the roughness of rocks and turns them into smooth stones, Our Lord too can smooth out the roughness of our grief if we allow ourselves to be gently submerged in the peace he offers. Anne Morrow Lindbergh wrote,

> I do not believe that sheer suffering teaches. If suffering alone taught, all the world would be wise, since everyone suffers. To suffering must be added mourning, understanding, patience, love, openness and the willingness to remain vulnerable.[27]

Jesus can offer us all these things. He can quench our thirst and teach us to come out of grief as a person who is more loving, compassionate, grateful, and peaceful than we have ever been before. This is what we truly thirst for in our grief. This is what God alone can give us.

Try This

Just as a hug, pat on the back, or squeeze of the hand can wordlessly give comfort, we can feel divine comfort through sacred touch. A man being prepped for a dangerous surgery once asked the priest at his bedside, "Father, do you have a rosary?" The priest pulled out his rosary and asked, "Do you want me to pray with you?" "No," the man replied. "I just want to hold it."

Touching or holding a religious object can be like holding God's hand during your most difficult moments. It is praying by touch. Consider slipping a small crucifix or rosary in your pocket. Set a statue of Jesus by the side of your bed, where you can reach it in the darkest hours. Keep a cross in your desk drawer, to pick up when you feel alone. God is there in the touch.

Lifting My Cross

Dear Jesus,
The cross of my grief is so much heavier than I thought it would be.
Did you feel that way when you carried your cross
to Calvary?
Some days I feel like I cannot possibly carry it
another step.
So I ask you, please, to help me.
I know I should not complain.
I try not to feel sorry for myself.
I look at what you suffered for us, and I am overwhelmed by your love.
But I am afraid grief has changed me.
I have lost such a special person in my life.
Now I don't know how to be who I once was.

Please wrap me in your love, and show me how to
become the new person I must be.
I place all my sorrows, complaints, and frustrations at the
foot of your cross.
I beg you to make them lighter for me
so that I can take them up for another day and follow
you as you have called me to do. Amen.

CHAPTER 10

Forgiving Our Sorrows

Carl sat in the dark, slumped on the floor, holding the phone. He wanted to throw it across the room. He would have if it were not an expensive new iPhone. His sister-in-law had just called to tell him his brother was dead. Dead! Out of nowhere, in the middle of the night, he got this news! He hadn't even known his brother was sick. Apparently his sister-in-law didn't think it was important enough to call him, several days before, when his brother had a heart attack.

Anger consumed him. He and his sister-in-law had never gotten along well, and it had driven him and his brother apart. They rarely talked. He hardly knew his nieces and nephews. It didn't help that he and his family lived on the other side of the country. But Carl always believed they would get together again sometime. Like old times. Have some fun. Share some laughs and good memories. They had talked about planning a fishing trip—just the two of them—when they both retired in a few years. And now this! Carl banged his fists on the floor and gave himself up to gut-wrenching sobs.

So Many Sorrows

Death brings with it many sorrows. The immediate loss can be complicated by countless other factors. We may have had an unfinished fight with the person who died. Maybe we're upset by how medical or emergency personnel handled a situation. We may disagree with family or friends, who share the same loss but want to handle it differently. Other people can hurt us with the things they say. We may be carrying some completely unrelated anger that resurfaces because we are weak with grief. We may be mad at ourselves. Maybe we're mad at the world. All of these hurts, piled on top of our grief, can make it unbearable. At some point, we need to slowly examine each piece of our angry puzzle and figure out the best way to deal with it.

Little pieces may be the easiest to release. After my grandpa died, I was mad at the world. It was the first major death in my lives. I resented strangers who were happily going about their life without the burden of grief my family had. This is an example of an unrealistic anger. We can release this kind of anger by realizing that most people don't know about our grief. It's not their turn to grieve.

Then there are the people who try to comfort us but fail. With these it might help to remember St. Paul's advice: "Be kind to one another, compassionate, forgiving one another as God has forgiven you in Christ" (Ephesians 4:32). People who have not gone through a grief like ours will try to be compassionate, but still, they might say or do stupid things. They may bog us down with stories of someone else's tragedy. They may pry or offer unhelpful suggestions. It's not their fault. We did the same thing before we knew grief. After my dad died, I realized how badly I had failed my best friend when her mother died. At that time, I had no idea what it felt like to lose a parent. I didn't know grief could hurt so much. I was insensitive to her pain.

The next level of anger may be directed at someone who didn't do things the way we thought they should have been done at the time of the death. With prayer and compassion, we should put ourselves in their shoes. We can ask ourselves how we would have handled the situation had we been in their place. Journaling about it could help. Here it's most important to remember the teaching of Jesus: "Stop judging and you will not be judged. Stop condemning and you will not be condemned. Forgive and you will be forgiven" (Luke 6:37).

Finally, we may have to forgive ourselves or our departed loved one for some unfinished business that is leaving us with unresolved anger. We may think this is a burden we will now carry forever. But just because a person is gone, that doesn't mean we can't apologize to them or forgive them. We can still talk to them. We can have this conversation with them in our hearts or on paper. It's never too late to forgive or to be forgiven.

The Hard Work of Forgiveness

Some sorrows may seem unforgivable. Murder, suicide, and medical malpractice can fall into this category. Through Our Lord's own witness, we are called to forgive, no matter how hard it is. In his final hours, Jesus forgave the criminal on the cross. After his resurrection, he forgave Peter for his denial.

Chuck's wife was killed by a man who tried to steal her purse. Chuck's grief was heavily laced with an angry need for revenge. The morning of the trial, he was so distraught that he went to Mass first to pray for strength. The Gospel reading was about forgiveness. "Peter . . . asked him, 'Lord, if my brother sins against me, how often must I forgive him? As many as seven times?' Jesus answered, 'I say to you, not seven times but seventy-seven times'" (Matthew 18:21-22). Chuck counted. The word "forgive" was used more than fifteen times in the liturgy that day, including the powerful words of the Our Father, "forgive us our trespasses as we forgive those who trespass against us." He realized that God had inspired him to go to Mass that morning, not to strengthen him for the fight, but to call him to give up the fight and forgive.

Forgiveness, however, is not a onetime thing. It's a work in progress. Rarely can we forgive once and be done with it. The pain comes knocking again and again. We must stop opening the doors of our minds to this negativity. We must not allow the story into our heads, to be played over and over again. Forgiveness means a constant and conscious refusal to dwell on the hurt. We do not repress it. We admit it is there. But we don't let it live any longer in our hearts.

This is hard work. Old anger will catch us off guard when we least expect it. Forgiveness is almost impossible for us to do alone. We need God to be there, guiding us through the tough spots. That's one reason why Pope Francis called upon the entire Catholic Church to celebrate a Year of Mercy in 2015. He wrote, "At times how hard it seems to forgive! And yet pardon is the instrument placed into our fragile hands to attain serenity of heart. To let go of anger, wrath, violence, and revenge are necessary conditions to living joyfully."[28]

How wise our Holy Father's words are! As long as we have grudges of any kind, we won't be able to recover fully from our grief. There is a healing power in forgiveness. Forgiveness replaces pain with peace. Forgiveness calms the body, mind, and soul. If we find it hard to forgive, we may want to turn to a person who had so much to forgive—Mary, the mother of Jesus.

Our Lady of Sorrows

God chose Mary to give birth to his Son but also to witness the terrible death of that Son, to hold his lifeless body in her arms, and to grieve the loss of his earthly presence in her life. Her human heart had many sorrows to forgive. In fact, one of the titles for Mary is Our Lady of Sorrows.

It's said that Mary suffered seven great sorrows in her life. All of them would be difficult for an average person to forgive. Mary's sorrows are listed as:

1. The prophetic words of Simeon to Mary, when Joseph and Mary presented the infant Jesus at the Temple: "You yourself a sword will pierce" (Luke 2:35). We might ask, "Who would say something like that to me?"

2. The flight into Egypt. How scared and angry would we be if we had to flee our home?

3. The loss of Jesus in the Temple. We can imagine how mad we would be at our own child for disappearing like that.

4. Seeing her son carrying the cross. How upset we can be over any pain or suffering inflicted on our loved ones!

5. The crucifixion. We may carry anger over the death of our loved one, but none died as Jesus did.

6. The piercing of the side of Jesus with a spear. The way we or our departed one was treated even after their death can fill us with rage.

7. The burial of Jesus. Funerals and burials can leave us full of regrets and bad memories.

Having known all these sorrows, Mary surely can show us how to let go of any anger. Pope Francis wrote, "God did not wish to leave humanity alone in the throes of evil. And so he turned his gaze to Mary, holy and immaculate in love (cf. Ephesians 1:4), choosing her to be the Mother of man's Redeemer."[29] In Mary, God has given us the perfect companion and guide to lead us out of bitterness and into forgiveness. If God chose her for himself, we can choose her too.

In 1809, Pope Pius VII composed a lengthy litany to Our Lady of Sorrows. His titles for Mary included Mother Sorrowful, Mother Tearful, Mother Consumed with Grief, Mother Most Sad, Fountain of Tears, Mirror of Patience, and Strength of the Weak. When we have much to forgive and when grief makes us weak with anger, Mary can truly be our strength. As the *Catholic Catechism for Adults* confirms, "[Mary] prays for us, loves us, and always bring us to Jesus."[30]

Try This

Your grief can be much more difficult to handle if it's complicated by the need to forgive some hurt, pain, or resentment. Consider going to Reconciliation. Whether you are mad at God or at any of his children, going to him for reconciliation will help.

Our Lord tells us, "Forgive and you will be forgiven" (Luke 6:37). This also works in reverse. If you let God first forgive you, you will find it easier to forgive others. In the Gospel of Luke, Jesus says to a sinful woman, "Your sins are forgiven. . . . Go in peace" (7:48, 50).

To find peace from angry grief, seek out a priest you know and trust. Or visit a parish where you are unknown. Most parishes post times for Reconciliation on their website. You can also make a personal appointment with a priest, especially if it has been a long time since you have been to Reconciliation. Find a good priest to help you feel God's forgiveness wash over you and settle into your heart. Then you will be ready to forgive others.

Forgive My Anger, O Lord

Dearest Father,
Grief brings so many negative emotions.
I sometimes feel anger, resentment, jealousy, or bitterness.
It seems I am often mad;
mad at others, mad at myself, mad at my dear one who
died, even mad at you.

These are feelings I do not want.
They are not part of the person I want to be.
I want to forgive and forget, but I'm not very good at it.
Please give me the grace to release all the real and imag
ined hurts.
Help me to stop going over the same resentments again
and again.
Open my heart to new stories;—
stories of love and joy,
stories of goodness and compassion,
stories of peace and forgiveness.
When I am failing at this, please remind me that you have
given me your beloved mother
—Our Lady of Sorrows—to help me through this pain.
May your gentle mother show me how to welcome a little
joy, acceptance,
forgiveness, and compassion back into my heart.
Thank you, most forgiving God.
I trust in you. Amen.

CHAPTER 11

The Gift of Faith

It was all a blur. It seemed as if George had just left when two policemen were standing at her door saying there had been an accident. They told her they would take her to the hospital. In a state of shock, she grabbed her purse and allowed herself to be gently helped into the patrol car. The officers had no answers for her questions. So she sat in the backseat and mumbled Hail Marys to herself over and over again.

At the hospital she got the news. George had had a massive heart attack and driven off the road. Paramedics said he was dead by the time they got there. Fortunately, no one else was hurt. Her children began to arrive. At some point, they left the hospital and took her home. There they argued about who would stay the night with her. But she insisted she didn't want anyone. If they stayed, they would make her go to bed. All she wanted to do was sit in her rocker and say her Rosary.

Tested

People often say it was only their faith that got them through the loss of a loved one. When we look back over the days surrounding the death, we often realize we never would have had the strength to do what we did without the grace of God and the support of prayers. I know I felt the power of prayer working in my life when I was forced to make impossible decisions and face terrible realities as my dad was dying. It is then that we know faith is a great gift.

Faith can help us through a death, but our faith can nevertheless be challenged by death. We might be tempted to abandon God because it feels as if he has abandoned us. Our Lord's own disciples sometimes felt this way. Once, when some were leaving him, Jesus asked Peter if he wanted to go too. Peter answered, "Master, to whom shall we go? You have the words of eternal life. We have come to believe and are convinced that you are the Holy One of God" (John 6:68-69). Let us remember Peter's words.

Jesus promised us, "I am the light of the world. Whoever follows me will not walk in darkness, but will have the light of life. . . . I came into the world as light, so that everyone who believes in me might not remain in darkness" (John 8:12; 12:46). Notice that Jesus did not promise we would never have darkness, but he did promise that he would lead us out of the darkness. It's said that we need darkness to see the beauty of the stars. We also need some darkness in our lives to experience the true beauty of God's love.

Sometimes we may think that people who have great faith do not or should not grieve. This puts unnecessary pressure on a faithful person to suppress their grief. Being a person of faith does not shield us from grief. But we have resources to handle it. We have God!

Pope St. John XXIII shows us this by the way he handled his own grief when, as a young seminarian, he found his beloved pastor dead on the floor before morning Mass. The shock and loss had a profound impact on him. While he took comfort in knowing he would see his friend again in heaven, he still experienced all the symptoms of grief. He complained of being distracted in prayer and wrote in his journal, "This is my greatest sorrow. . . . I do not know how to behave. . . . I no longer know how to live in a world which has become strange to me. . . . I need a fresh start." Through the sadness and confusion, he clung to his faith, writing, "O Jesus, you alone can see how heartbroken I am." And on another day, "Jesus is still here and opens his arms to me, inviting me to go to him for consolation." [31]

Finding God

If we are having trouble finding God in our grief, we have to remember to be still. Often when we are troubled by grief, we like to surround ourselves with noise. We may leave the television or radio on. We may keep ourselves so busy that we don't have time to think. We may avoid the quiet at any cost. But it is in the quiet that we find God.

Elijah learned that lesson while waiting for God on the mountaintop. First there were strong winds, then an earthquake, and then fire. But God was not in any of these. God was only in a light gentle sound that brushed Elijah's heart (see 1 Kings 19:11-13). So it is with us. We may not find God in all the noise of death, the funeral, and grieving. But if we can be quiet, we will find him.

We are promised this over and over in Scripture.

The Lord is with you when you are with him, and if you seek him he will be found; but if you abandon him, he will abandon you. (2 Chronicles 15:2)

Those who seek the Lord lack no good thing. . . .
The Lord is close to the brokenhearted,
    saves those whose spirit is crushed. (Psalm 34:11, 19)

God is our refuge and our strength,
    an ever-present help in distress. (Psalm 46:2)

And I tell you, ask and you will receive; seek and you will find; knock and the door will be opened to you. (Luke 11:9)

Although God is near to us, he will not break down our door. He is a God who sits quietly and patiently outside the door of our hearts and waits for us to open that door to him. If we keep the doors and windows locked, we will never connect with God. We will be missing out on the most amazing healing power in all the world. Thomas à Kempis tells us, "Look to God's love as the most important thing in life. If you keep God at the center of your life, you will easily overcome all other things."[32]

When it comes to opening our hearts more fully to God, we can't just crack a window. We must throw open all the doors. We want to let the light of God's love wash over every bit of gloom and darkness. The way to fully open our hearts is with silence, spiritual reading, and prayer. These are the three most important building blocks of faith.

Even when we don't have time for extensive prayer, we can frequently whisper the simple prayer Padre Pio wrote: "Stay with me, Lord."[33] Although he wrote this as a prayer to be said after Communion, we can say it whenever we need Our Lord's healing presence in our life.

Moving Mountains

Faith is more than just believing in God. It is having confidence in him. It is trusting his words to his disciples: "Amen, I say to you, if you have faith the size of a mustard seed, you will say to this mountain, 'Move from here to there,' and it will move. Nothing will be impossible for you" (Matthew 17:20).

Jesus didn't promise we could move a mountain immediately. We may only move a mountain a few small rocks or a couple of big boulders at a time. But with faith, we can begin to move any mountain, including the mountain of our grief. That is better than sitting in despair and staring at the same old mountain for the rest of our lives.

God will not move the mountain for us. We have to take some action ourselves. St. James tells us, "Faith of itself, if it does not have works, is dead" (2:17). The work of grieving begins with opening our hearts to the inspiration of God. The more we let our faith guide our actions, the more we will find God reaching out to help us along this journey.

The steps we take towards recovery may be different for each of us. Yet one way or another, we need to begin to move forward. We need to learn how to ease ourselves back into life—picking up work we may have left undone, resuming friendships we may have ignored. We need to allow ourselves to smile, to laugh, and to enjoy life again.

In his book *Between Heaven and Mirth*, Fr. James Martin, SJ, asserts, "Joy, humor, and laughter show one's faith in God."[34] We can begin to laugh and be happy again because we trust in God. We know that our loved one is okay. We know we will be together again in heaven. This faith is a reason to smile. Failing to gradually embrace some joy and lightheartedness in the midst of our grief can be a sign that our faith is not strong enough. We have not yet opened our hearts to the healing only God can give us.

In severe cases of grief, a step we may need to take is to seek out a grief counselor or a spiritual advisor. There is no shame in this. We are simply letting God work—as he often does—through other people. If we feel this is a step we need to take, it's important to choose a counselor who has a background in our faith. Otherwise, a counselor could inadvertently undermine our growing relationship with God or fail to realize the importance God plays in our healing. Faith-based counselors can be found through Catholic Charities and diocesan offices.

Try This

Increase your prayer time. Scripture tells us, "Is anyone among you suffering? He should pray" (James 5:13). The more you are suffering, the more you need to pray. Some say that the veil between heaven and earth becomes thin when we experience a death. We can become more closely connected to God because we still feel connected to our loved one, who is now in God's hands. Thus this is an especially good time to pray a little more than you ever have before.

Begin by setting aside the same time every day for prayer. This helps to make prayer a habit. Most people prefer early in the morning, before anything else can get in the way. Just set your alarm for fifteen minutes earlier than you usually do.

Next, find a prayer routine that inspires you. You might want to begin by reading Scripture for five minutes. Then sit quietly for five minutes, and listen to what God is saying to you in that reading. Say a few favorite prayers if you wish.

Finally, respond to God by writing a prayer letter to him in your journal. These fifteen minutes of prayer can make an amazing difference in your day and your life.

Walking in Faith

Dear Lord,
Thank you for the gift of my faith.
I don't know how I could face my grief without you walking with me.
Even when I feel alone, I call out to you, believing that somewhere in the darkness, you are near.
I need you, dearest Lord, to be my light—the light that guides my steps.
I'm afraid—anxious and unsure of what I should say or do or even feel.

I have mountains to move, big changes to accept, and
new directions to explore.

Help me feel you alive in my soul, filling me up like a
balloon and keeping me afloat.

Help me turn to you when I am afraid, confused, or just
feeling sorry for myself.

Inspire me to find more time to be quiet with you.

Let me draw closer to you and find peace in
your embrace.

In all things, teach me to rely on my faith in you,
never forgetting that it is the gift that makes me strong.

Thank you for that, dearest God. Amen.

CHAPTER 12

Souls and Saints

Dennis almost threw away the invitation to a special All Souls' Day Mass for those who had lost a loved one in the last year. Those grieving would sit in reserved seats and process forward to light a candle at the foot of the altar in memory of the one who had died. Dennis didn't like sitting in a reserved seat or processing up to the altar. Nor did he think the loss of his ninety-six-year-old mother merited the same kind of recognition as the loss of a spouse or a child might merit. Let those people go to this memorial Mass.

Still, he didn't pitch the invitation. He set it on his desk, just in case. Every time he saw it, he reminded himself why he didn't need to go. But one thought kept creeping in: Mom would like it if he went. This was her kind of thing. And so he reserved a spot. He sat with the others who were grieving, he lit the candle for his mom, and he felt more at peace than he had since her death.

Rituals of Remembering

Rituals help us come to peace with death. Early in human history, people mounded stones or built elaborate pyramids to honor the dead. Today we light candles, place flowers on a grave, plant a tree, or leave an empty chair at the table. We may carry a memento in our pocket, place a bit of hair in a locket, or wear a loved one's medal. We celebrate All Souls' Day, Memorial Day, and special anniversaries.

Different rituals will help different people. We should embrace the rituals that are meaningful to us without criticizing others for their rituals or allowing others to criticize us for ours. For example, people of European descent may celebrate All Souls' Day with a quiet Mass and candle lighting. However, those of Hispanic descent may celebrate the same day, which they call *Dia de los Muertos,* or "Day of the Dead," with a picnic at the grave site—complete with the deceased's favorite foods and music.

Our personality type and family traditions can also play a role in what memorial practices we find most helpful. Some people find great peace in visiting a grave. Others may never go. The experiences of Mary Magdalene and the mother of Jesus can give us some insight in this regard. Both women stood at the cross. Both women were beloved by God. But only Mary Magdalene ran to the tomb on Sunday morning. Scripture never says that Jesus' mother went. Some believe she didn't need to go because, as soon as Jesus left the tomb, he went to visit her. She already knew he was risen and no longer in the grave. Whether we go to a grave or stay home, Jesus will find us and comfort us, just as he did for both his mother and his dear friend.

Whatever rituals we choose to follow, we need to ask ourselves if they are bringing us peace or causing us to stay stuck in our grief. Rituals should help us let go. If our rituals are causing us to cling to the deceased, we must remember Our Lord's words, "Let the dead bury their dead. But you, go and proclaim the kingdom of God" (Luke 9:60).

We may think it's a sign of great love that we cannot let go of the one who has died. However, it can be a sign of selfishness. Our rituals should help us establish a new relationship with the one who is gone, not yearn for the old relationship. In grieving for his own wife, Christian writer C. S. Lewis observed,

> How wicked it would be, if we could, to call the dead back! . . .
> Could I have wished her anything worse? Having got once through death, to come back and then, at some later date, have all her dying to do over again? They call Stephen the first martyr. Hadn't Lazarus the rawer deal?[35]

C. S. Lewis knew that those who are deceased are in a much better place than earth can ever be. We need to let them go in peace.

Not Lost

When we speak of a person who has died, we often say we lost them. Although this is an extremely common way for those of us who are grieving or those who comfort us to avoid the dreaded "d" word, it is in reality not true. For people of faith, deceased people are not lost. We know where they are. They are in the hands of God. At the end of the Catholic funeral liturgy, we entrust them to God with these beautiful words: "Receive her soul, O holy ones; present her now to God most high."

Even though our faith tells us our loved one is with God, we still may long for confirmation. Sometimes we may be blessed with a dream or a sign that our loved one is in heaven. The night my dad died, I dreamed I opened a door and saw him playing cards with all of his old buddies who had died before him. He looked at me and said, "Close the door. You can't come in here." It has been my only dream of him, but it gives me peace that he is where we spend our whole lives hoping to be. However, not everyone has a dream like this.

We may worry about whether our loved one is in heaven or purgatory, especially if we see purgatory as a place of suffering. The *Catechism of the Catholic Church* tells us not to worry. Purgatory is not a place of suffering; it's a place where we prepare to meet God. "The Church gives the name *Purgatory* to this final purification of the elect, which is entirely different from the punishment of the damned" (1031).[36] We shouldn't think of purgatory as a torture chamber. Rather, it's a dressing room where we can put on our very best selves to meet our Creator. The *United States Catholic Catechism for Adults* further assures us, "The Communion of Saints includes the faithful on earth, the souls in Purgatory, and the blessed in heaven."[37] All are in God's hands. All are saints in the making.

We may seesaw between asking our deceased to intercede for us before God and offering Masses for the peaceful repose of their souls. Pope St. John XXIII did the same thing. He wrote of his beloved pastor, "Even in the other life he watches over me and shows his kindness as if he were still alive." But in the very next paragraph, he writes how deeply he is praying "for the soul of my parish priest, that he may rest in peace." It is not for us to know exactly where anyone is on their eternal journey to God. It's enough for us to know that God is caring for them more than we ever could. The pope goes on to tell us, "Jesus the Savior is much more anxious than we are for the salvation of souls. . . . His grace will not be lacking when the moment comes for their conversion. This moment will be one of the most joyful surprises of our glorified souls in heaven."[38]

Being Saints

Knowing our loved ones are with God can inspire us to better prepare ourselves to meet our Savior. We may think more about our own death and about our priorities in this life. We may consider putting our affairs in order and letting our last wishes be known. This does *not* mean that we are going to give ourselves over to dark thoughts, give up, or even consider suicide! (In fact, if we have suicidal thoughts, we should immediately seek the help of a mental health professional.) But somehow, when we know someone special is waiting for us on the other side, the idea of dying may not be so frightening. It may prompt us to look forward to the day when we too may be a saint in heaven, even though we know our work here on earth is not yet finished.

Wanting to be a saint may sound like an arrogant goal. All those who go to heaven are saints, however, even if the Church has not canonized them. Committing ourselves more strongly to becoming a saint can help us through our grief. Saints are people who have drawn close to God. They are people who pray. They are people who study the word of God and seek to spend time with him. They are people who love and serve others for the sake of God. Interestingly, whenever we do any of the above, not only are we becoming saints, but we are pulling ourselves out of our grief.

In his apostolic exhortation On the Call to Holiness in Today's World, Pope Francis tells us that anyone can be a saint.

> To be holy does not require being a bishop, a priest or a religious. We are frequently tempted to think that holiness is only for those who can withdraw from ordinary affairs to spend much time in prayer. That is not the case. We are all called to be holy by living our lives with love and by bearing witness in everything we do, wherever we find ourselves.[39]

Even though the Holy Father says people do not have to withdraw from ordinary life to be holy, this is often what happens to us for a time while we are grieving. We withdraw from our normal activities. It might be one reason we feel closer to God during our period of grief. Yet even as we heal, we can continue to maintain and grow in this holy closeness.

Accepting the pain of our loss is another way to grow saintlier. Jesus taught us, "Store up treasures in heaven, where neither moth nor decay destroys, nor thieves break in and steal. For where your treasure is, there also will your heart be" (Matthew 6:20-21). Our treasure is in heaven. It is where our hearts are. It is where we too hope someday to be.

Try This

Music is often associated with the joy of heaven: harps softly playing, angels singing, quiet violins and cellos. This is not surprising. Music can soothe the soul, wash away sorrow, and help us feel closer to God. Yet many people find it painful to listen to their usual music after a death. Special songs can be too emotional.

Instead, consider listening to something different. Try liturgical music, Christian rock, or classical or instrumental music. One woman who had always loved the symphony found new joy in country music! When grief overwhelms you, good music can relax, heal, and inspire you. It can even make you smile.

In Your Arms

You may personalize this prayer by using the name and appropriate gender pronoun for the individual you are lifting up to God:

Heavenly Father,
You have someone very dear to me in your loving arms
right now.
I'm not sure if they have awakened yet to all the wonder
of being home with you.
If not, please let them see you soon in all your glory.
Open their eyes to the beauty of heaven.
Let them be filled with the peace and joy of being forever
with you.

Please give them a special hug from me.
Tell them I am grateful that they are free of all worry
and pain.
Let them know I will be okay.
I miss them so much, but I know they are happier
with you
than they could ever be back here on earth.
I am grateful that they are with you, even though
some days
my longing for just a few more minutes together is
almost unbearable.
Especially during my sad moments,
I look forward to the day when I can come into your
arms too, O Lord,
and be reunited with all those who were once in my arms
and are now in yours.
Until then I entrust my loved one to you.
Help me do my best to earn admittance too into your
heavenly kingdom.
Thank you for the gift of my loved one and the time we
shared. Amen.

CHAPTER 13

Choosing Gratitude

We were test-driving a new car. "Where should I go?" I asked my husband as I got behind the wheel.

"Where do you want to go?" he asked.

Immediately an answer popped into my head. To my dad's house. Dad was a great car buff. We always took our new cars over to show him. But now tears choked me. Dad had been gone for over a year, and I still thought of him every day. Mostly now the memories were just little teasers: a passing thought about something we had done, he had said, or he had given me. But today, jumping up in front of me was a huge, unexpected hole—a thing I would never be able to do again: take a new car over for my dad to see.

I realized I was at an emotional fork in the road. I easily could have collapsed into tears, but along with the sadness, a sense of gratitude wrapped itself around me. I almost felt as if Dad was in the car with me, giving his approval for the purchase. I felt grateful for all the wisdom he had given me over the years about driving and evaluating the strengths of a car. I drove in a new direction.

We Have a Choice

It's a good sign of healing when we can come to the crossroads of a memory and realize that we have the choice to be sad or to be grateful. In the early stages of grief, we often have little control over our emotions. The slightest thing can bring us to tears. But when we reach a point at which we can choose, it's always best to choose gratitude. Tears may still pool at the corners of our eyes, but we don't have to give in to them. We reach beyond the loss and grab on to gratitude. Gratitude can heal. It helps us move through life with a better attitude.

As we go forward in our grief, we may begin to relate to the famous words of Alfred Tennyson in his poem "In Memoriam": "'Tis better to have loved and lost / Than never to have loved at all." Tennyson wrote the lines of this classic poem after the sudden death of one of his best friends.

It's sometimes true that the greater our love for a person, the more we may grieve their death. It helps to realize that the reason we are grieving so deeply is precisely because we were so wonderfully blessed to have such a good person in our lives. We wouldn't want to change that. If, in the midst of our grief, we can look with gratitude on the life we shared, we will eventually mourn less the days we won't have. This kind of gratitude is not easy. It takes time. But it can be very healing.

When we're in the midst of great grief, it's easy to become jealous. We look at happy families, happy couples, or happy friends and feel a sense of anger or envy. Instead, we need to start looking at those who never had a love like we had—whether with a spouse, child, parent, sibling, friend, mentor, or coworker. We need to realize how very blessed we have been.

Right after a loss, our grief is often uncontrollable. But in time, grief can become a habit. One way to break that habit of sadness, bitterness, or withdrawal is through gratitude. Throughout Scripture we are called to be grateful. The angel

Raphael told Tobit and his son, Tobiah, "Bless God and give him thanks before all the living for the good things he has done for you" (Tobit 12:6). And King David commanded the people, "Give thanks to the LORD, who is good, / whose love endures forever" (1 Chronicles 16:34). The psalms frequently repeat King David's call to be grateful.

Our Lord offers perhaps the most powerful reason to turn to God in gratitude. When he heals the ten lepers, only one returns to thank him. We can hear the sadness in his words when he asks, "Ten were cleansed, were they not? Where are the other nine? Has none but this foreigner returned to give thanks to God?" (Luke 17:17-18). Even in our grief, let us not be one of the nine who fails to give thanks to God for the blessings he has given.

Which Comes First?

St. Paul also gives us a strong command to be grateful: "Rejoice always. Pray without ceasing. In all circumstances give thanks, for this is the will of God for you in Christ Jesus" (1 Thessalonians 5:16-18). This three-part teaching can leave us with "the chicken or the egg" kind of question. Which comes first? Rejoicing? Praying? Giving thanks?

When we are grieving, we may be tempted to say that we cannot give thanks because we're not rejoicing. However, St. Paul's instructions offer a grab bag of options, with any one of them leading to the others. So if we do not feel like rejoicing or giving thanks, we can pray. And prayer will lead us to give thanks and to rejoice. Joy, prayer, and gratitude are always braided together, twisting around each other in a lovely blend of goodness—a perfect guide for our life.

We should also pay close attention to the words St. Paul chose. He didn't say, "For all things, give thanks." Rather, he said, "In all circumstances give thanks." In other words, we are not called to be grateful *for* our loss, but we are called to be grateful *even in the midst* of our loss.

One way to feel more gratitude, even in our grief, is to remember the story of our loved one. Telling the story is important, and that is why a wake, where we can speak about the deceased, is a critical part of the funeral process. We need to tell others, over and over again, what happened. It helps us come to terms with the reality and to accept it. It's a way for us to honor our loved ones and speak of how good they were. And it gradually helps us see those things for which we can be grateful. If we refuse to talk about our loss or our grief, it's harder for us to find reasons to be grateful.

We should continue to tell the tale until we feel we have come to peace with it. We can write the story of our loved one in a journal. This can be a powerful healing tool to help us move forward. Or we can tell friends or family we need to talk about our loss. People may avoid talking to us about it because they are afraid to open the wound again for us. But if we tell them we need to talk, those who are close to us are usually happy to listen. We could also join a grief support group, in which people come together regularly to tell their stories of loss. Telling the story leads to healing and gratitude.

All Is Gift

Another way to increase our sense of gratitude is to realize that all is gift. Every moment of our lives is a gift from God. Everything we have is a gift from God. Every dear person in our lives is a gift given especially to us from the hand of God. It is all gift! We get credit for nothing. Even our pain and suffering can be gifts. They may open new possibilities before us. They help draw us closer to God. They show us how to be more compassionate with others.

Every person is a lovely gift from God. We did nothing to deserve them or to earn them. Scripture tells us,

> The earth is the LORD's and all it holds,
>   the world and those who dwell in it. (Psalm 24:1)

When we open our eyes to the fact that everything belongs to God, we begin to see how generously he has showered good gifts upon us. We can then also begin to trust that God will continue to give us the gifts, resources, people, and experiences we will need to go on. As St. Paul writes,

> Have no anxiety at all, but in everything, by prayer and petition, with thanksgiving, make your requests known to God. Then the peace of God that surpasses all understanding will guard your hearts and minds in Christ Jesus. (Philippians 4:6-7)

When we are not so afraid of the future, we may be more able to find peace in the present. We may become more grateful that our loved one is now in God's hands.

Blessed Solanus Casey was a Capuchin Franciscan who believed in the power of gratitude. For over twenty years—from 1924 to 1945—he served as the porter at St. Bonaventure Monastery in Detroit. He was well-known for his humility and for praying for people in need of healing, hundreds of whom claimed to have been cured. Crowds lined up outside the monastery doors just to have him pray with them. He always encouraged people to "thank God ahead of time." His holy life is a testimony to the importance of always thanking God. Maybe we should begin now to thank God for healing us of our grief and opening a new future before us.

Try This

Practice being more grateful. The commercial world constantly reminds you of what you don't have. This feeling of want is magnified when you experience a great personal loss. Thus it's always good to remember the blessings you do have.

Try naming ten things each day for which you are grateful. You can write these in a journal, say them on the first ten beads of a rosary, or even count them on your fingers before you fall asleep each night. Or write a story of your loved one's life, recording the memories for which you are most grateful. Or simply say thank you to others more often. Say thank you to anyone who helps you in any way. Say thank you to

God for even the smallest blessings. Cultivate more gratitude in your life, and soon a lovely garden of peace and contentment will grow.

Giving Thanks

This is a "fill-in-the-blank" prayer, which means there are places for you to say whatever comes to mind. As you do this, be aware of the ideas God may whisper in your heart about blessings you have not considered or remembered.

My great God,
I thank you.
I know I have not thanked you enough.
But right now, being grateful is sometimes difficult
for me.
It's hard to be thankful when I am sad.
Yet I know you have never left my side, and I
appreciate that.
I thank you for the greatest blessings in my life, which
include _____.
I thank you for the little blessings of this day, which
include _____.
I thank you for the gift of faith, which has helped me
to _____.
I felt your grace alive in my life today
when _____.

I ask you, please, to open my eyes more fully to all the many blessings of my life right now.

Remind me of how good my life has been.

Help me concentrate more on what I have rather than on what I have lost.

Encourage me to recognize new blessings.

Help me trust that you are leading me from my grief and into something good.

For that I thank you, my ever-generous God! Amen.

CHAPTER 14

Blessed Are We

Shortly before my dad died, a terrible accident made headlines in our city. During an ice storm, a tractor trailer slid off an overpass and crashed onto the highway below. Amazingly, the driver wasn't hurt. When asked what he was thinking as his truck was flying out of control, the man said all he thought was "This is going to hurt." That story stuck with me as I faced my final days with my dad. I knew it was going to hurt to lose him. I was going to miss his wisdom and his joy.

He must have known what I was thinking, because one day he said to me, "You know I'm going to die soon, but I don't want you to be sad. I had a good life. I'm ready to go. I don't want you to cry." I smiled at him and said, "I know, Dad, but I'm still going to cry."

I was prepared for Dad's dying to hurt. I was not prepared for all the blessings that would flow into my life in the midst of the sorrow. I never expected the graces I received.

We Will Be Comforted

We all know the beatitudes—they're the basis of Our Lord's Sermon on the Mount. In them Jesus said that eight types of people would be blessed. Six of these are the meek, the merciful, the peacemakers, the righteous, the poor in spirit, and the clean of heart. We all strive to live as such people.

But two of the beatitudes are about conditions we do not welcome. Jesus said we are blessed when we are persecuted and when we mourn. "Blessed are they who mourn, / for they will be comforted" (Matthew 5:4). None of us want to mourn. But now here we are, mourning. The good news is that Jesus not only promised we would be comforted, but he concluded the beatitudes by saying, "Rejoice and be glad, for your reward will be great in heaven" (5:12).

When we think about the many human traits and conditions Our Lord could have talked about up on the mountain, it's amazing that he singled out those who mourn. This tells us that God has a special place in his heart for us when we are grieving.

Pope Francis has stressed the importance of the beatitudes in Christian life: "The Beatitudes are like a Christian's identity card. So if anyone asks: 'What must one do to be a good Christian?' the answer is clear. We have to do, each in our own way, what Jesus told us in the Sermon on the Mount."[40] The pope goes on to tell us we should not ignore our mourning.

> The worldly person ignores problems of sickness or sorrow in the family or all around him; he averts his gaze. The world has no desire to mourn; it would rather disregard painful situations, cover them up or hide them. . . .
>
> A person who sees things as they truly are and sympathizes with pain and sorrow is capable of touching life's depths and finding authentic happiness. He or she is consoled, not by the world but by Jesus.[41]

Pope Francis assures us that we will be able to feel the healing touch of Jesus when we embrace our sorrow. We are blessed when we mourn, because Jesus is close. We can sense him near. We can ask him to sit with us when we cannot sleep, comfort us when we cry, lead us to a new normal.

Sometimes in life, we may feel as if we are praying to a distant or unknown God. But in the midst of grief, God invites us to know him as fully as is humanly possible. It's almost as if this invitation to greater closeness to him is his sympathy card to us—his memorial gift to us in honor of our loved one. This is a blessing.

Feeling His Mercy

St. Faustina, the religious sister whose visions of Christ led to what has become known as the Divine Mercy devotions, frequently said that God permitted suffering in our lives so that we might turn to him and know his mercy. Certainly, feeling God's mercy and love can be one of the blessings of our grieving process. Often, as we begin to be comforted, we realize it is God who is the power and the force behind our healing.

When a fond memory of my dad crosses my mind, I now see it as a gentle touch from God. It reminds me that I was blessed to have Dad in my life. He was a good man, and he is now happy with God. He's no longer suffering. For that I am grateful. Even though I now have the pain of grieving, I would rather have that than continue to watch my dad in physical pain. I don't have to endure my emotional pain alone, though, because Jesus suffered to take on all the hurt and suffering of the world. I can find peace by taking the pain of my grief to Jesus and placing it upon his altar.

Our God truly is a God who seeks us out in our mourning, simply to wrap us in his mercy. Let us look again at the story of Jesus coming to Bethany after his good friend Lazarus died. The way the story unfolds, Martha goes out first to meet Jesus. After she talks with him, she goes back into the house and tells Mary, "The teacher is here and is asking for you" (John 11:28). Before Jesus went to shed his own tears over his deceased friend, he was there comforting the sisters. In the same way, he is waiting for us to come to him. He is asking for us.

God wants to pull us out of our grief. When we are grieving, we often spend too much time looking backwards. We look backwards because we don't want to forget or because we cannot imagine our lives without the one who is gone. Adult children talk of feeling like an orphan when the last parent dies. When a spouse dies, men and women often say a part of them has died. No wonder we don't want to look forward.

God wants to turn us around. He's right beside us, ready to lead us forward. He's offering us his hand, his mercy. He's calling us to remember the words Moses spoke to Joshua shortly before he died, leaving Joshua to lead the Israelites into the Promised Land: "It is the LORD who goes before you; he will be with you and will never fail you or forsake you. So do not fear or be dismayed" (Deuteronomy 31:8). Our loved ones surely want to tell us the same thing. From heaven they are whispering to us, "Open your heart to God's mercy. It's amazing!"

Called to Listen

Even though God wants to show us his great mercy, he isn't going to force himself on us. We must be willing to listen for his whispering in our hearts. At first, we may not even realize he's there. We are like Mary Magdalene, wandering around in the garden where Jesus was buried. She didn't recognize Jesus, even when he asked her, "Why are you weeping? Whom are you looking for?" (John 20:15). She thought he was the gardener. It was only when Jesus called her name that Mary knew him and fell at his feet. God is calling our names too. But we must listen for him.

"God does not hide himself from those who seek him with a sincere heart," Pope Francis has said.[42] But like Mary Magdalene, we have to go out and look for God. We won't find him in the things of this world. Our normal activities won't bring us comfort. Nor will we find God if we think we can just cover up our grief by trying something new or going someplace different. New people, places, and things won't bring us peace, unless they are activities that lead us to God.

C. S. Lewis discovered this in his great grief. "All that is not eternal is eternally out of date," he wrote.[43] So where do we find that which is eternal? One of the surest ways is through Sacred Scripture. We will hear God speaking most directly to us through the Bible. We may think we already know the Scriptures: we hear them proclaimed at Mass, and we may have studied the Bible in school or as part of a Bible study program. But when we are grieving, we hear things we never heard before.

Further, when we pick up the Bible, we will find passages that are never declared in the normal readings of the Mass.

We also come to understand God's word in a new way because of our experience with death and grief. Words that may have once rolled over us with little or no impact now become lifesavers to which we cling. They open our eyes to the reality of God's goodness, and they give us inspiration to move forward. St. Paul encourages us to "let the peace of Christ control your hearts" and to "let the word of Christ dwell in you richly" (Colossians 3:15, 16). We will learn to love God's word in a whole new way when we read it with grieving hearts.

Try This

Make more time for Scripture reading. Turn off the TV, and read Scripture before you go to bed. Or take a Bible with you when you know you're going to be somewhere that requires waiting. If you can't find time for daily Scripture reading, try to schedule time on weekends, during lunch, or on an evening once a week. You may want to read a selected book from beginning to end. Biblical books that speak to the heart of grieving people include the Psalms, Job, the prophets Jeremiah and Isaiah, and the Gospels of John and Luke.

Or you may want to read the daily readings selected by the Church. You can access these on the website of the United States Conference of Catholic Bishops (usccb.org). There you can sign up to have readings sent to you daily by e-mail or delivered to your iPhone, or you can listen to the readings through iTunes.

Listening for Your Voice

You may want to tuck this prayer into your Bible, to say before you begin your Scripture reading:

Dear Lord,
I long to hear your voice!
I need you to whisper your words into my heart.
I believe your promise that I will be comforted.
I believe you are the only source of my comfort.
I trust that if I can hear you, then I will be consoled.
But sometimes I do not hear.
I feel lost and alone.
It seems that you are silent.
I need to hear your voice, Lord.
Nudge me, so that I find the right time and the best place to sit quietly with Scripture.
For I know it's there that you can be heard.
It's there that you speak for all times and to all peoples.
Guide me to the passages in the ancient texts where I will find what I need for today.
Let me hear your words in a new and uplifting way.
Please bless me and comfort me with your holy message.
I want to hear your voice. Amen.

CHAPTER 15

Glorious at Last

Maria was nervous about talking to Fr. Joe. It wasn't the funeral plans that worried her as much as the question she must ask. Shortly before her husband, Art, became sick, he had argued with his old friend Henry. The friends never patched up their disagreement, and the sicker Art became, the madder he got at Henry. "I don't want that man at my funeral," he said. "If he can't come to see me now, there is no sense him coming when I'm dead. You tell him that, Maria!"

Maria never argued. She knew her husband was venting his anger over his failing health, displacing it onto his old friend. But now she was worried. Should she honor her husband's dying wish? But how could she tell Henry he wasn't welcome at the funeral?

After listening to her dilemma, Fr. Joe smiled and said, "Maria, there's no anger or bitterness in heaven. Jesus washes all that away the minute he opens his arms to welcome us. It's the mystery of God. Your husband is a new man now. He doesn't care at all about some silly old argument. Art is full of God's mercy, love, peace, and joy now. He would want Henry to be at his funeral."

Embracing the Mysteries

Life is full of mysteries, a constant moving forward into the unknown. With each day, we leave something behind, and we enter into something new and unexpected. Why we receive different joys and sorrows is a complete mystery; it often seems we deserve neither the blessings nor the sadness. This is the story of every life. While we take these little mysteries in stride, the mysteries of death can overwhelm us. That is when we might want to consider the Rosary.

Mysteries are at the heart of the Rosary—the Joyful, Luminous, Sorrowful, and Glorious Mysteries, which tell the story of Our Lord's life. They remind us of how both Mary and her divine son lived, suffered, died, and rose above the pain. We may not understand the mystery of their lives any more than we understand the mystery of our own. But we embrace it.

St. Thérèse of Lisieux felt that her life unfolded in three parts, similar to the three classic sets of mysteries of the Rosary. She called her early childhood her Joyful Mysteries—a time when God gave her "a father and mother more worthy of heaven than of earth."[44] But after her mother died, when Thérèse was very young, she entered into the period she called her Sorrowful Mysteries. She wrote, "All my gaiety went after Mother died. I had been lively and open; now I became diffident and oversensitive, crying if anyone looked at me."[45] For ten years she wallowed in grief and depression, spoiled and pampered by her father and older sisters. Yet she never stopped praying and reflecting on the life of Jesus.

Her grieving came to an end, she said, after Midnight Mass on Christmas Eve in 1886. She referred to this as her Christmas miracle.

The Divine Child, scarcely an hour old, flooded the darkness of my soul with radiant light. By becoming little and weak for love of me, He made me strong and full of courage. . . .

That glorious night, the third period of my life began, the loveliest of all, and the one in which I received the most graces. In one moment, Jesus . . . accomplished what I had been trying to do for years. . . .

Charity took possession of my heart, making me forget myself, and I have been happy ever since.[46]

Thérèse called these last years of her life her Glorious Mysteries.

Our grief may not leave us in one miraculous moment, as hers did for St. Thérèse, but when we sincerely seek to draw closer to God, our lives will mysteriously begin to lose their sorrow and become glorious again. We will begin to see the beauty that shines forth when storm clouds are pushed away by the radiant beams of the Son.

A Prayer for Peace

The Rosary is one of the best prayers to help us find peace in the midst of grief. Throughout the centuries, many saints and popes have encouraged us to pray it, including Pope St. John Paul II. In 2002, he marked the twenty-fifth anniversary of his pontificate by declaring a Year of the Rosary:

The Rosary is by its nature a prayer for peace, since it consists in the contemplation of Christ, the Prince of Peace, the one who is "our peace" (Ephesians 2:14). Anyone who assimilates the mystery of Christ . . . learns the secret of peace. . . . Moreover, by virtue of its meditative character, with the tranquil succession of *Hail Marys*, the Rosary has a peaceful effect on those who pray it, disposing them to receive . . . that true peace which is the special gift of the Risen Lord.[47]

At this time, the pope also added a new set of mysteries to the Rosary, the Luminous Mysteries, which he called the Mysteries of Light.

More powerful than the message of an apostolic letter is the message of Mary herself, who has appeared several times over the centuries to encourage the faithful to pray the Rosary. Mary appeared to St. Bernadette Soubirous at Lourdes in 1858, for example—an apparition that has been deemed credible and worthy of belief by the Church. Bernadette said that Mary carried a rosary with a gold chain and white beads and that the Blessed Mother prayed the Rosary with her.

In 1917, Mary appeared several times to three young children at Fatima. On her July 13 visit, she told them, "Pray the Rosary every day in honor of Our Lady of the Rosary to obtain peace in the world." One of the visionaries, Lucia Santos, became a Carmelite nun and lived for eighty-eight years after the appearances of Mary, dying in 2005. She often said, "There is no problem, I tell you, no matter how difficult it is, that we cannot resolve by the prayer of the Holy Rosary."[48]

Needing Resurrection

When Pope St. John Paul II introduced the Luminous Mysteries in 2002, he suggested a schedule for praying the various mysteries. The Glorious Mysteries should be said on Sunday and Wednesday, the Joyful on Monday and Saturday, the Sorrowful on Tuesday and Friday, and the Luminous Mysteries on Thursday. This, however, is not a hard-and-fast rule; it is only a recommendation. We are free to pray whatever mysteries seem most appropriate and helpful to us on a given day.

When we are in mourning, we may originally find comfort in praying the Sorrowful Mysteries. Reminding ourselves of how Jesus suffered can help us realize we all must have some pain in our lives. If God did not spare his only Son from suffering, how can we expect that he would spare us? We must not, however, let ourselves get stuck on the sorrowful end of the Rosary.

If we want to heal from grief, we should spend some time with the Luminous Mysteries. With the five Mysteries of Light, we are reminded of how Jesus can bring light to our darkness:

1. Through his Baptism. Are we not promised that Jesus is God's beloved Son?

2. Through his miracles. He changed water into wine at the wedding feast in Cana. Can he not also change our sorrow into joy?

3. Through his preaching. What powerful messages of love does he have for us now?

4. Through his Transfiguration. Even in his glory, Jesus reaches down to us and says, "Rise, and do not be afraid" (Matthew 17:7).

5. Through the Holy Eucharist. Does he not offer his very Body and Blood to nourish us through every struggle?

These are powerful mysteries for us to meditate on as we work our way through our grief.

But mostly we need the Glorious Mysteries. We need a resurrection. We need to meditate fully on the fact that Our Lord and Savior rose from the dead and ascended into heaven. We need to remember that he sent the Holy Spirit down, to shower us with gifts that could get us through anything. We need to think about heaven, about Mary waiting there with her Son for us, about her identity as the gracious Queen of Heaven. When we turn our thoughts to the glorious, it will be easier to let go of our sorrow.

While reflecting on the Glorious Mysteries, we might want to imagine what it's like for our loved one to now be with Jesus, Mary, angels, saints, deceased friends, and family. What will our loved one look like? Surely no more aches and pains; no glasses, wheelchairs, or oxygen hoses; none of the crooked bones or scars we remember; maybe younger or maybe older. One legend says that everyone will be thirty-three in heaven, because this is the age Jesus was when he died. Others say we will get to pick our age, or we will be ageless. None of this matters. What matters is that we and they will be glorious! This is what we all live and die for. It's worth some grief and suffering to become what God always meant us to be: radiant with his love.

Try This

Part of the process of healing from grief involves moving beyond our own needs to think of others. Gently and mindfully praying the Rosary for a wide variety of intentions can help us do that. To expand your Rosary meditation, pick a different intention for each Hail Mary you pray. If possible, connect your intentions to the mystery of that decade. Is someone joyfully awaiting the birth of a baby? Does someone need to come back to the light of the Eucharist? Is someone in sorrowful agony? Does someone need the glorious gifts of the Holy Spirit? Pray for people like these as you pray the Rosary, and your own burden of grief will not seem so heavy.

Living in Mystery

Dear Lord,
The mysteries of life overwhelm me.
I want to understand, but I do not.
Through the mysteries of your own life,

I know we all must experience joy and sorrow, grief
and glory.
Yet please don't leave me forever wrapped in the beads
of sorrow.
Open my eyes to all that is glorious.
Help me become more aware of the joy in my life.
Help me soak up the light of your love.
Let all my loved ones who have died be completely
washed clean
of all that was painful, difficult, and negative here
on earth.
Let them bask in your radiance.
It gives me peace to picture them with you.
Please guide, protect, and inspire me until the day I can
join you there.
I am ready to come when you call.
But with your grace, I will finish the work you have
planned for me here on earth.
With you by my side, I will walk courageously
through the mysteries that remain in my life.
Thank you, great God, for being with me through
it all. Amen.

CHAPTER 16

The Light of Hope

Sherry woke up and stared at the ceiling. It was Saturday, and she had no reason to get out of bed. Nor did she feel motivated to do so. Since Russ had died, her life was dreary and dingy. She didn't open windows or make the bed. She hardly did any cleaning. But this morning, she felt restless—not listless but restless. She wanted to do something. But what?

Suddenly she threw back the covers and jumped out of bed with more energy than she had had in weeks. She was tired of this. She needed some light in her life. She threw open all the windows. She walked out onto the patio to enjoy the sunrise. She noticed for the first time that the gardens she and Russ had once tended and enjoyed together were now full of weeds and ruin. She quickly ate breakfast, then headed to the garden shop, where she picked out the loveliest flowers she could find. She worked all weekend restoring her gardens and bringing blooming beauty back into her life. Sometimes she cried. But often she found herself humming. And by Sunday night, she realized that she felt better than she had in months.

The Power of Beauty

"What does it mean that Jesus is risen?" Pope Francis asked in his Easter message in 2013. "It means that the love of God can transform our lives and let those desert places in our hearts bloom. The love of God can do this!"[49]

When we're grieving, we live in a desert place. We're thirsty. We're like the deer by the stream, spoken of in Psalm 42 and often depicted in cathedral windows and religious art:

As the deer longs for streams of water,
    so my soul longs for you, O God.
My soul thirsts for God, the living God. (Psalm 42:2-3)

The image is a promise that we will find the One for whom we thirst.

When we grieve, we thirst for the one who has died, even though we know we cannot have them back. Often we don't know what we want instead. We may lock ourselves away, thinking nothing can satisfy us, but eventually thirst overwhelms us. We feel overcome with the need for light, beauty, food, activity, or someone to talk with us. In reality, what we really need is God. Because God is all of that. He is light. He is beauty. He is food for our soul. He is the activity in our hearts. He is someone to talk with. He is our true and only hope.

We thirst for beauty because it can heal. It can transform. It can lift our spirits. Flowers bring beauty to a funeral, but our grief is too raw then for us to appreciate them. Only weeks or months later do we find that we're ready for flowers, music, laughter, and sunrises to fill our lives and wash away our grief. We are ready for God to bring back the beauty.

Thomas Merton, the Trappist monk and writer, knew grief. His mother died when he was only six. He missed her greatly.

When his father remarried, Thomas went to live with his mother's family. Despite the grief of his early life, Merton later wrote, "[There is] nothing dead that cannot live again in the presence of His Spirit. No heart so dark, so hopeless, that it cannot be enlightened and brought back to itself."[50]

Merton was merely stating, in a different way, what God says to everyone:

> See, I am doing something new!
>   Now it springs forth, do you not perceive it?
> In the wilderness I make a way,
>   in the wasteland, rivers. (Isaiah 43:19)

God Is in Charge

Hope includes the feeling that Someone greater than we are is in control, the knowledge that everything will work out—even if we don't know how. Hope gets us out of bed in the morning and inspires us to plant a garden, play the piano, or do other beautiful and healing things. To have hope is to have one of the three theological virtues. The seeds of these virtues—faith, hope, and charity—are planted in our hearts by God. He waters them by his grace. They grow strong in the light of his love.

The Church tell us, "Hope assures us that, with God's grace, we will see our way through what now seems such a daunting challenge. For believers, hope is not a matter of optimism, but a source for strength and action in demanding times."[51]

When we have hope, we surrender our pain and worries to God. We believe his promise: "I know well the plans I have in mind for you, . . . plans for your welfare and not for woe, so as to give you a future of hope" (Jeremiah 29:11).

Anthropologists have found evidence that even the earliest peoples hoped in some kind of god or creator. They didn't know God's name, but they still felt Someone Greater than They was out there. They believed and hoped in God as they understood him, turning to him to send the rain, to provide food, and to calm the storm. Hope is still planted in our hearts today. But now we are blessed to know the source of this hope—to know God's name, to know his Son.

Knowing God exists is not enough. What brings us hope is knowing that God cares. Even before Jesus suffered and died for us, the Israelites knew this:

> The LORD's acts of mercy are not exhausted,
>   his compassion is not spent;
> They are renewed each morning . . .
>   . . . I will hope in him.

> The LORD is good to those who trust in him,
> to the one that seeks him. (Lamentations 3:22-25)

Fr. Pierre Teilhard de Chardin was a Jesuit priest and renowned paleontologist who, as a scientist and a priest, had a unique perspective on God. His beautiful prayer, "Patient

Trust," gives us good advice for putting our hope in the God
who has always been and will always be:

> Above all, trust in the slow work of God.
> We are quite naturally impatient in everything
>   to reach the end without delay.
> We should like to skip the intermediate stages. . . .
>   as though you could be today what time . . .
> will make of you tomorrow. . . .
> Give Our Lord the benefit of believing
>   that his hand is leading you,
> and accept the anxiety of feeling yourself
> in suspense and incomplete.[52]

Hope for Today

It would be easier if hope were like a dependable high-beam
flashlight that could lead us quickly and permanently out of
our grief. But instead, hope is a flickering candle. Sometimes its
light is bright. Sometimes it's weak, or it seems as if it has gone
out. While we would prefer the strong, dependable flashlight, a
candle is much more beautiful. It has a soft dancing glow that
can bring us peace. We don't use high-beam flashlights to cre-
ate a sense of calm and comfort in our lives. We use candles.
God gives us this kind of glowing hope. Even when it seems as
if our wick of hope has gone out, we know that God will be
there to light it for us again.

When we have God by our side, we don't need a hope that lights up the entire path before us. We only need enough hope to get us through the next few hours. We don't have to ask God to dump a bucket of hope on us. We only need enough for today.

Pope St. John XXIII was great at making spiritual "rules" for himself. These are scattered throughout his journals and essentially are simple daily goals. (In a similar way, we can write our own goals as we strive to grab just enough hope for a day.) Pope John's ten most inspiring rules have become known as his Daily Decalogue, each of them beginning with the encouraging phrase "Only for today."

As we strive to replace grief with hope, here are two of the pope's rules that might be helpful:

- Only for today, I will seek to live the livelong day positively without wishing to solve the problems of my life all at once.

- Only for today, I will have no fears. In particular, I will not be afraid to enjoy what is beautiful and to believe in goodness.[53]

Early in the Gospel of Luke, Jesus stands up in the synagogue in Nazareth and reads from the scroll that is handed to him. The words he reads are from the prophet Isaiah. Luke only records that Jesus read the first part of the passage, which proclaims,

"The Spirit of the Lord is upon me,
  because he has anointed me
    to bring glad tidings to the poor.
He has sent me to proclaim liberty to captives
  and recovery of sight to the blind,
    to let the oppressed go free,
and to proclaim a year acceptable to the Lord." (4:18-19)

Those of us who grieve might like to believe that Jesus finished reading that section of Isaiah, affirming that he had come

to comfort all who mourn. . . .
To give them oil of gladness instead of mourning,
  a glorious mantle instead of a faint spirit. (61:2, 3)

What we do know is that after reading the scroll, Jesus proclaimed, "Today this scripture passage is fulfilled in your hearing" (Luke 4:21). He promised that he would be our hope, but the people of Nazareth rejected him. They couldn't believe that a man with whom they were so familiar could work such wonders. Let's not make the same mistake. Let's not turn our backs on the oil of gladness or the glorious mantle God promises to all who mourn.

Try This

Take a "hope" inventory. Make a list of things that bring you hope. This might include activities you enjoy, good friends, or dear family members. Then make a list of things that tax your hope. This might include too much time alone, overeating in front of the TV, or reading too much braggadocio on Facebook posts.

Now plan one way to spend more time with what feeds your hope and less time with what dampens your hope. This might be as simple as deactivating your Facebook account and using the time you usually spend there to take a walk and pray the Rosary. Just one simple switch from something hopeless to something hopeful can make a big difference.

Lantern of Hope

Holy Spirit,
Please be the lantern of hope in the midst of my grief.
Let me see even a glimmer of the good and the beauty
that are still present in my life.
Let me see that you are planning a future full of hope
for me.
Surround me, please, with family, friends, and even
strangers who can give me hope.
Introduce me to new possibilities.
Give me strength to undertake activities that will energize
and inspire me.

Gently lead me forward when I am tempted to stay right where I am.

When I worry too much and forget to follow you, please be the spark that gets me going.

When I get bogged down trying to paddle alone through dark, muddy pools,

please light my way to fresh, bubbling streams.

Fill me with hope—even if it is only enough for today.

Then, everlasting Font of Hope, light the flame of my hope again tomorrow

if my tears and sorrow should extinguish it.

For this I thank you, great Spirit of God. Amen.

CHAPTER 17

What to Keep

After Dad died, we needed to clean out our family home. We took clothing and household items to various charities. My siblings and I, our children, and our grandchildren took the items that were special to us, and we tagged furniture and knickknacks for a garage sale. The night before the sale, my brother carried Dad's big wooden rocker to the garage. This was the chair Dad always sat in, facing the front door, waiting for my visit. "Isn't anyone taking the rocker?" I asked in disbelief.

A quick survey of my siblings found that no one had room for it. Although I didn't know where I'd put it, this chair called to me, and so my brother helped me load it into my car. When I got home, my husband helped me carry it upstairs and into an already overcrowded office. At first, I would sit in the chair when I wanted to feel close to my dad. Eventually, I rearranged the family room, and now his grand old rocker has a place of honor by our fireplace. There are some things you just can't give away.

Less Is More

It's a huge responsibility to sort through the bits and pieces of another person's life. It's also a very personal and sometimes spiritual experience. We may find items we never knew existed. We may wish to hear a story that will no longer be told about a memento hidden in the back of a drawer. We may discover a deeper faith than we expected—a rosary in a jacket pocket, a prayer card in a wallet, a medal on a chain. These can be ways God makes himself known to us in our grief.

There is no right or wrong way to do this work, as long as we do it. Clutter can be a source of stress in our lives. It hangs over our heads and adds to the burden of our grief. Holy shrines are beautiful places to visit, but it's not good to make a shrine from the pieces of another person's life. As St. Thérèse wrote, "Joy does not reside in the things about us, but in the very depths of the soul."[54]

Keeping everything is neither healthy nor responsible. It will hold us back in our healing, and on some level, it can even be a form of selfishness if the items could be used by the poor. St. Basil the Great, an early bishop of the Church, stressed Our Lord's command to care for the needy: "The coat unused in your closet belongs to the one who needs it; the shoes rotting in your closet belong to the one who has no shoes."[55] It's healing and right for us to think of the poor as we sort through the possessions our loved one no longer needs.

When it comes to questions of what to keep, less is often more. Pope St. John XXIII kept only pictures of his deceased family members. He said the pictures, always sitting on his bedside table, reminded him of all the cherished people who were waiting for him in heaven. He did find comfort in taking just one book as a memory of his beloved childhood pastor. He wrote in his journal that he had taken,

> as a precious token of remembrance of my priest, his *Imitation of Christ*, the same volume he had used every evening

since his seminarist days. To think he became holy, poring over this little book! This will always be my dearest book, and one of my most precious jewels.[56]

Things Are Just Things

Sorting through a loved one's possessions might be easier if we remind ourselves that things are just things. Psalm 115 mocks those who make gods out of material things:

Their idols are silver and gold,
   the work of human hands.
They have mouths but do not speak,
   eyes but do not see.
They have ears but do not hear,
   noses but do not smell.
They have hands but do not feel,
   feet but do not walk;
   they produce no sound from their throats. (115:4-7)

In the same way, the things our loved one left behind have no feelings. We must avoid turning these possessions into idols. Certainly the one in heaven doesn't need or care for this stuff any longer. They don't expect us to keep all of it.

In his encyclical on Care for Our Common Home, Pope Francis warns us about becoming too attached to possessions. He encourages us to strive for "that simplicity which allows us to stop and appreciate the small things, to be grateful for the opportunities which life affords us, to be spiritually detached from what we possess, and not to succumb to sadness for what we lack."[57]

The detachment Pope Francis speaks of reflects the detachment of his namesake, St. Francis of Assisi. In writing the rule for the Franciscan way of life, St. Francis said the friars shouldn't own anything, because possessions can be a cause of disputes that hinder us from loving God and neighbor. Thomas of Celano, one of the first to follow Francis, wrote, "Francis' greatest concern was to be free from everything of this world, lest the serenity of his mind be disturbed even for an hour by the taint of anything that was mere dust."[58] We're not called to the beggarly life Francis lived, but we might find the same peace of mind Francis found if we're less attached to material things.

Attachments to or arguments over possessions can intensify our grief and disturb our peace of mind. It's important to remember that our loved one is not in the possessions. Our loved one lives in our heart, not in things.

Even if we give away everything a person had, we won't forget the person or ever stop loving them. We have a special place for them in our hearts, and we'll keep them safely there for all time. This is much better than confining them to cardboard boxes, overstuffed closets, and basement shelves. As we sort through all their stuff, it might help to remember the wisdom of Sirach:

> Do not let your hand be open to receive,
> but clenched when it is time to give. (4:31)

Let's store our great memories in our heart but generously give away the physical things that we don't need.

Questions to Ask

It's impossible and unwise to keep everything a loved one left behind. Keeping only a few things makes those items even more special and cherished. But what should we keep?

It's often easier to start with small items, like jewelry and medals. My dad kept the religious medals his mother always wore, but I never knew that until he gave them to me a few years before he died. I put them in a small frame, wrote an explanation of their significance on the back, and now keep the frame on my desk. Christmas ornaments might also be something you want to keep. I kept one of my mother's glass ornaments for my granddaughter who was born a few weeks after my mother died. I wrote a note saying it was a gift from her great-grandmother, whom she may have passed on her way from heaven to earth.

Sorting through larger items no one wants or things *everyone* wants can be more challenging. Start with a prayer for strength and guidance, and then consider these questions:

1. **Does a family member or someone close to the family have a practical need for this item?**

2. **Who might cherish it for sentimental reasons?**

3. **Who—beyond the scope of immediate family and friends— might need it?**

4. **Can this be shared?** If the deceased person had an abundance of something—such as books, collectibles, or tools—we might ask several people if they would each like one of these things as a remembrance of the person. This can relieve us of the temptation to keep too much for ourselves and allows a greater number of people to have a tangible reminder that will spark warm memories.

5. **Do we already have our own special mementos?** The things our loved one gave us can mean more than the things we take. One morning years ago, my dad stopped by my house unexpectedly to give me a small wooden statue he had seen at a garage sale. He thought I would like it. I cherish that gift more than anything I could have taken after he died.

6. **How much time and effort will it take to maintain this item that I'm considering keeping?**

7. **Do I really want this, or am I keeping it out of a sense of obligation?** We shouldn't let ourselves be burdened with things that don't bring us joy. If we feel an obligation, it's good to remember that material things now mean nothing to those in heaven.

8. **Can I make something different from this?** Many people make memory quilts from favorite articles of clothing. My brother made an amazing clock out of Dad's collection of pocket watches. Each watch, set at a different time, represents one of the hours.

9. **Am I strong enough to make this decision now?** Some things might need to be set aside until our grief is not so raw. It's okay to take our time.

Try This

Take pictures of things you want to remember but don't need to keep. You can also photograph deteriorating items, like old newspaper clippings, portraits, and letters. Photos are much easier to store than "stuff." Plus, modern technology lets us enjoy the photos as background or screen savers on our computers. It always makes me smile when I walk into my office and see a picture of my mother's china or one of the miniature cars my dad built over the years. The pictures on the computer screen stir lovely, ever-changing memories that I enjoy more than some item stashed away in a box, basement, or storage unit.

Wisdom to Let Go

Holy Spirit,
I need your help sorting through the things my loved one
has left behind.
Please send me your wisdom, and help me make
good decisions.
Inspire me to know what I should carry with me on my
journey of life
and what I should leave behind.
Wash away any guilt or sadness I may attach to things.
Help me remember that my loved one now has all they
may ever want in the arms of God.
It's not my job to keep things that are burdensome
for me.
Let me be generous and gracious in sharing what has
been entrusted to me.
Guide me to give to others what they need or can use.
Help me keep only what I truly cherish and need.
Give me patience when others push me to give or to keep
in ways that do not seem right to me.
Help me remember that things are only things.
The true treasures are in my heart.
For that I thank you forever. Amen.

CHAPTER 18

Filling the Hole

Daniel wasn't happy as he watched a new family move in across the street. To Daniel, the house would always be Henry's house, even though his friend had recently passed away. Henry had been a good neighbor. When Daniel's wife died two years before, Henry was the one who got him through. The old guy just seemed to know when to show up at the front door with two cold beers in his hand.

But now it was a tattooed father and his two young boys who were heading across the street! "Quite a tattoo you got there," Daniel said a bit snidely as he opened the door. He had no intention of making friends with this family. The young father stretched out his arm, displaying a pink ribbon surrounded by daisies. "In memory of my wife," he said. "She died of breast cancer when the boys were just toddlers. It's just me and the boys now. I was wondering if I could borrow a screwdriver until I get my tools unpacked."

Daniel felt something crack inside him. It was the wall he had built around his heart. For the first time in years, he felt sympathy for someone besides himself. At least his wife had not died until their children were all grown. "Come on in," Daniel said, in a jovial voice he had not used in a long time. "Happy to help. What are your boys' names?"

"Joseph and Henry," the young father replied.

A Lump of Clay

The death of a loved one leaves us with a great hole in our lives. Now that someone who once gave shape and structure to our lives is gone, we may feel like a listless and worthless lump of clay. However, we are a lump of clay in God's hands.

God once led the prophet Jeremiah to a potter's house so that Jeremiah could visually see the work a potter does. Then God told Jeremiah, "Like clay in the hand of the potter, so are you in my hand" (18:6). God gave Isaiah the same message. The prophet prayed,

> Yet, LORD, you are our father;
> we are the clay and you our potter:
> we are all the work of your hand. (Isaiah 64:7)

Even as we grieve, God is waiting to mold a new life for us. In his mind, the Divine Potter sees something life-giving for us.

Just because someone very special to us has died, that doesn't mean our work here on earth is complete. God still has a task for us; we're not the one who died. We need to ask God what his plan is for us now.

Since we are not doing the things we once did with or for the person who has died, some of us may find we have more time on our hands. Others, however, may discover we have less time than before, as we now do the work our loved ones once did. Either way, our season of grief is a good time to redefine ourselves and reexamine our priorities. We do that best by going to God. We should offer to him the lump of clay that is our life and ask him what he wishes to do with it now. We can do this during morning prayer, a weekday Mass, Scripture reading, or journaling.

Pope Francis tells us that, in order to be transformed, "we must first belong to God, offering ourselves to him who was there first, and entrusting to him our abilities, our efforts, our struggle against evil and our creativity, so that his free gift may grow and develop within us."[59] By offering to God the time and the gifts we have to share, we can be assured he will change our grief into something that is good and beautiful, not only for us but also for others.

Works of Mercy

Wednesdays were the hole in my life after my dad died. That was the day I always spent with him, doing whatever he needed. I prepared food and took him to doctors, to visit Mom in the nursing home, to the bank, and to the grocery store. When he was gone, I felt lost on Wednesdays. I told a friend I needed a new corporal work of mercy.

The corporal works of mercy are inspired by the Gospel story of the Last Judgment. We all know this parable. God calls the sheep to his right side and says, "I was hungry and you gave me food, I was thirsty and you gave me drink, a stranger and you welcomed me, naked and you clothed me, ill and you cared for me, in prison and you visited me" (Matthew 25:35-36).

In his apostolic exhortation On the Call to Holiness in Today's World, Pope Francis calls this judgment story "The Great Criterion."

> We cannot forget that the ultimate criterion on which our lives will be judged is what we have done for others. . . .
>
> Those who really wish to give glory to God by their lives, who truly long to grow in holiness, are called to be single-minded and tenacious in their practice of the works of mercy.[60]

Maybe the act of mercy we feel called to do is to "weep with those who weep" (Romans 12:15). Pope Francis praises this kind of ministry: "Knowing how to mourn with others: that is holiness."[61] However, God doesn't call every person who grieves to weep with others. He may call us to some new ministry. This is why we need to pray in order to discern our personal call. At the marriage feast of Cana, Mary told the stewards, "Do whatever he tells you" (John 2:5). This is good advice for us too. When the servants did what Jesus told them, he turned water into wine. In a similar way, if we do what Jesus tells us, we can make a small miracle for someone else.

St. Elizabeth Ann Seton is a good example for us. She didn't become the patron saint of those who grieve because she sat in her house and cried about being a widow with five young children. She became a saint because, despite her grief, she still opened her heart to God and others. She established a school for girls. She gave free education to those who could not pay. She founded the first religious order for women in the United

States, designing a habit for them that looked very much like the expected dress of a widow in mourning. She followed the command of the Gospel landowner who, despite the lateness of the day, says to us, "'Why do you stand here idle all day?' . . . 'You too go into my vineyard'" (Matthew 20:6, 7).

Making a Change

In cases in which a death is overwhelmingly tragic, people may be motivated to do something grand to make a change. They organize annual walks to fund research into cures for devastating diseases. They host golf tournaments to help a family whose young parent has died. They establish scholarship funds to assist promising young people like their loved ones who have died.

Doing something that makes a lasting change is a powerful way to redirect the anger and sadness of grief into something positive and life-giving. Now, we can't develop special events and new organizations for every person who dies. But we can do something small to change the life of someone else who is suffering—and this can help us find healing.

Mother Teresa once said, "Suffering . . . is a sign that you have come so close to Jesus that He can kiss you."[62] But Jesus doesn't just kiss us as we suffer through our grief; he also helps us become more sensitive to the suffering of others. He prepares us to go out and make a change. He teaches us to be kinder and gentler.

We may make a change by "picking up the mantle" and carrying on some good work that our loved one did. The idea of "picking up the mantle" comes from the Bible story of Elisha chasing after the fiery chariot that carried his beloved mentor, Elijah, up to heaven (see 2 Kings 2:1-14). When Elijah disappeared into the sky, his mantle fell to the ground. Elisha picked it up and set out to continue the work of the great prophet. Possibly our loved one too has left a holy mantle for us to pick up.

Likewise, the disciples who mourned Jesus' death didn't just sit around and mope for the rest of their lives. When the Holy Spirit came upon them, he inspired them to establish the greatest Church on earth. The Holy Spirit will come to us too and bring us the gifts and the inspiration we need to make a change, to do something beautiful and wonderful. We have to open our eyes to what is being dropped before us or whispered in our hearts.

There is an adage that says happiness is a door that opens outwardly, not inwardly. At some point on our grief journey, we need to open the door of our hearts and step out of our self-pity. When we do, we will begin to find happiness. When we work to change something for someone else, things will begin to change for us.

Try This

Read Pope Francis' apostolic exhortation On the Call to Holiness in Today's World. The Holy Father can truly inspire you to move beyond your grief into the joy of helping someone else. In all his works, he writes for the average person. His words are simple and beautiful—not stale or stuffy. Consider this:

True enough, we need to open the door of our hearts to Jesus, who stands and knocks (cf. Revelation 3:20). Sometimes I wonder, though, if perhaps Jesus is already inside of us and knocking on the door for us to let him escape from our stale self-centeredness.[63]

Francis' documents and other writings are available in book form at local Catholic bookstores, or they can be ordered online. They include Joy of the Gospel, *The Face of Mercy*, and On Care for Our Common Home. You can also find his writings, speeches, and homilies posted in several major languages on the Vatican website (w2.vatican.va), where you can download and read them for free.

A Prayer to the Potter

Heavenly Father, Divine Potter of my life,
I am just a sad and sorry lump of clay.
But I am yours.
Mold me into something new and good.
Inspire me to write something beautiful on the blank slate of my future.
Show me how to help others in the same way that others have helped me.
Send me out into your vineyard to do at least one kind and generous thing today.
I know how short life can be.

Help me to not waste the days I have left here on earth.
Help me make a difference, in memory of the one who
has made a difference in my life.
Let me carry you to someone who needs you.
Help me say and do the right things.
Inspire me to offer a smile, a prayer, or a helping hand.
Lord, please show me what goodness can fill the empty
hole in my life.
Help me do what you are calling me to do in this new
phase of my life. Amen.

CHAPTER 19

The Peace of Acceptance

The screen saver on my computer is a collection of pictures that cover a period of about ten years. Just a few days before the first anniversary of my dad's death, a picture of Dad popped up. Usually tears welled in my eyes when Dad, smiling and healthy, made an appearance on my screen. But this day was different.

The picture was the last one I had taken of Dad; he asked me to take it and send it to my siblings. It was the last time he had been able to get out of his hospital bed and sit in a chair. As I studied the picture—seeing his tired eyes, weak smile, and frail body—I was waiting for my tears to flow. But they didn't come. Instead, I was able to look at the picture with peace. I whispered to him that I was glad he was no longer suffering. I was glad he no longer had an oxygen tube rubbing his face raw and no longer had to wear a hospital gown.

I realized I had completely and totally accepted the fact that he was gone from my earthly life but was waiting for me in a life that would be, quite simply, heaven!

A Part of Us

Grief is not something we get rid of like the flu. It can become part of us. Fortunately, it usually gets better. Unfortunately, it may never go away completely. Just as we will never forget the person who has died, we will never forget our grief over losing them. We will remember how badly it hurt, even if we don't actually still feel the same pain. Like a physical ailment, grief can be acute or chronic. It's often acute in its early stages, then slips into a chronic condition of the soul. We learn to live with grief in the same way we might have to live with allergies, diabetes, or other chronic conditions. We learn to get it under control.

On rare occasions, some other major life event may bring grief back to us in an acute flare-up for a short period of time. Ideally, though, we learn how to hand our grief over to God and trust him to lead us forward. We learn to be grateful for the good memories and to let go of the painful ones. We learn to accept the fact that we won't see our loved one again in this life, but they are waiting for us on the other side. If grief doesn't lessen in twelve months, we should discuss it with a doctor or a qualified counselor.

In her classic *Frankenstein,* English author Mary Shelley wrote, "The time at length arrives when grief is rather an indulgence than a necessity."[64] She knew what she was talking about. Mary fell into a deep depression when her daughter died. She was haunted by nightmares of the baby. Although she wrote that grief was a choice, her own life story shows how challenging it can be to move from grief back to a healthy and balanced life. For this we often need help, and the best help comes from God. We can and must control the crying and the sadness, push it back to a reserved corner of our hearts, and get back into the stream of life.

To learn to accept grief in a healthy way, we might want to keep in mind these words of Isaiah:

Truly, the LORD is waiting to be gracious to you,
    truly, he shall rise to show you mercy; . . .
you shall no longer weep;
He will be most gracious to you when you cry out;
    as soon as he hears he will answer you. . . .
And your ears shall hear a word behind you:
    "This is the way; walk in it." (Isaiah 30:18, 19, 21)

As we move forward in our grief, we may have to remind ourselves every morning that God is leading us with his gentle words, "This is the way; walk in it." Grief may remain an undergarment for us, but eventually, we should begin to do as St. Paul recommends:

Put on then, as God's chosen ones, holy and beloved, heartfelt compassion, kindness, humility, gentleness, and patience, bearing with one another and forgiving one another, if one has a grievance against another; as the Lord has forgiven you, so must you also do. And over all these put on love, that is, the bond of perfection. (Colossians 3:12-14)

I like to use this passage as my "dressing prayer" every morning. For it was love that got us into our state of grief, and it will be love that will get us out.

Moving Forward

Our greatest challenge in grief can be acceptance. When we refuse to accept the death, we get stuck in some kind of no-man's-land where nothing seems right. This is where we suffer the most because there seems to be no direction in our life. Once we accept the fact that our loved one is not coming back, we realize we need to move forward. By accepting, we are opening our eyes to the light at the end of the tunnel.

Elisabeth Kübler-Ross, who devoted much of her life to studying death and dying, wrote, "The most beautiful people I've known are those who have known trials, have known struggles, have known loss, and have found their way out of the depths."[65] That is exactly what we are challenged to do. We can take as our motto the recommendation of St. Teresa of Avila: "We ought to make some progress, however little, every day."[66] Like most saints, Teresa of Avila knew grief. Her beloved mother died when Teresa was only eleven, and for a while, great grief paralyzed the young girl. But she learned to move forward—so well that she spent a good part of her life traveling around Spain and forming over a dozen new convents of Carmelite nuns.

St. Catherine of Siena is another saint who walked through grief. She lost several sisters and nieces to devasting plagues, yet in a letter to a friend, Catherine wrote,

It's my experience that for God's true servants, . . . when it's time to abandon their own consolation and embrace difficulties for God's honor, they do it. And when it's time to leave the woods and go to public places because God's honor demands it, they go.[67]

How, we might wonder, does leaving the woods of our grief and giving up the consolation of our sorrow help us honor God? It's simple. When we continue to wallow in grief, we show no trust in God. When we move forward, we honor God by showing we still believe in his goodness. We declare, through our acceptance, that God is still in his heavens and all is in his great hands.

St. Augustine of Hippo stated, "God created us without us: but he did not will to save us without us" (*Catechism*, 1847).[68] If we want to be saved from our grief, at some point we must take our own steps into a new life. God will always be there to help, but he will not pull us along unless we're willing to move.

The beautiful Serenity Prayer by Reinhold Niebuhr can motivate us. "God, give us grace to accept with serenity the things that cannot be changed, Courage to change the things which should be changed, and the Wisdom to distinguish the one from the other." We know that we cannot change death; it's irrevocable. We can't go back. We can go forward, or we can stay in the hole we have dug for ourselves.

It Is Peace I Beg of You

The beauty of moving forward is that it brings us peace. On the day she took her vows as a Carmelite nun, St. Thérèse of Lisieux carried with her a letter she had written to Jesus. It read in part: "May nothing in the world ever disturb my peace! O Jesus, it is peace I beg of you."[69] It is Jesus who can give us peace, but we don't have to enter a convent to find it. Jesus is the answer we seek, the resolution to our problems, and the peace our souls crave. We will find peace by accepting reality and letting go of our sadness.

As he was recovering from his great grief over losing his wife, C. S. Lewis wrote, "When I mourned her least, I remembered her best."[70] It's true that when we come to peace with our loss, the memories of our loved one actually become more precious and beautiful. In the midst of grief, we often can't think or talk about the one we lost. When we do think of them, the memories may be full of regret, the pain of their suffering, or the circumstances of their death. Our grief blocks the best memories. The sooner we can set aside our grief, the happier we will be. By accepting and letting go of grief, we are able to open ourselves up to better and more peaceful memories. Memories of the good times, the early years, the joy and the love, no longer make us cry. They make us smile.

St. Elizabeth Ann Seton wrote, "Nothing can be more pressing than the necessity for your peace before God."[71] In his great spiritual classic *The Imitation of Christ*, Thomas à Kempis tells us how to find that essential peace: "As soon as you yield yourself to God with your whole heart, not seeking this or that for your own pleasure or will but placing yourself entirely in his hands, you will find yourself quickly at one with God and at peace."[72]

We can surrender to God's will, as à Kempis advocates, when we understand the real purpose of prayer. It's not about telling

God what to do but about trusting that God always knows *exactly* what to do. It's learning to listen to God and accept his will and his grace in our lives. It's saying, as the young Samuel said, "Speak, LORD, for your servant is listening" (1 Samuel 3:9). When we can pray in this way, peace and acceptance will fill our hearts.

Try This

Imagery might help you let go of your grief. Imagine an open suitcase. Begin to put into that suitcase anything that's causing you pain. Put in the nights of crying, the sympathy cards you don't want to look at, the places you don't want to go. Put in the memories that haunt you, the painful words you remember, and the listlessness you feel. Pack this suitcase with all that you don't want anymore. Then imagine yourself closing and locking it.

Carry it out the door. Bring it to a place where it will be safe: maybe to the foot of the cross, to the arms of the Blessed Mother, to the steps of a beloved church, or up a high hill on a starry night. Leave it there for God to reach and take up.

Now imagine the freedom of turning your back on this heavy piece of luggage. Imagine walking away. Imagine taking a deep sigh of relief. Imagine feeling free. Imagine your body relaxing, your shoulders softening. Imagine feeling at peace. This is what giving your grief up to God can feel like.

Moving Forward

Heavenly Father,
I know it's time for me to move forward, to move beyond my grief.
Yet still I hesitate.
I struggle with acceptance.
And so I pause.
I thank you for the gift of my loved one who is no longer with me.
As I go forward without this one, could you please
replace my tears with lovely memories,
replace my sadness with a stronger belief in the glories of heaven,
replace my fears with trust in you,
replace my anger and frustration with forgiveness.
It gives me comfort to know that you hold my loved one in one hand
while you reach out another hand to me.
Through you, we are connected for all eternity.
Help me now to find my way in a world that is changed
but is still very blessed by you.
Help me be better rather than bitter.
Help me move forward with the simple peace
of acceptance.
I ask this through Christ Our Lord, who conquered death
and showed us the glory of resurrection.
Thank you! Amen.

CHAPTER 20

New Joy

My friend Jan was only forty when her mother died. Grief over-whelmed her. Although she had three precious young sons, for months Jan could not enjoy them. Her boys respected their momma's sadness, but they didn't know what to do when she cried, as she so often did. One day, looking through heavy tears at her somber twelve-year-old son—the comedian in the family—Jan said, "Oh, Todd, Momma is so sick and tired of crying. Do something to make me laugh!" Given license to once again be a happy child in a house weighed down by grief, Todd did a series of funny faces. In minutes Jan went from crying to laughing.

She says, "It was like he performed a mini miracle! He turned my whole world around in a minute. I was back to my normal happy self again." Years later, when Jan's dad and her sister died, Jan did not experience the terrible grief she had when her mom died. She said she had come to real-ize how precious life is and how important it is to be joyful, no matter what.

Inviting Joy to Return

When we lock joy out of our hearts for a long time, we may have to make a conscious effort to invite it back in. When we call for joy, it may come running like a happy child and jump right into our arms. But joy may also be a shy child, hiding in the corner, and may need to be gently and patiently coaxed to come to us. Joy may not feel right in making a return to our life, and we may not feel right inviting it back. However, no matter how difficult it may be, we must extend the invitation—over and over again, if necessary.

God doesn't want us to live without joy. He created the world to be a place of joy. Birds singing, the loveliness of dawn, the beauty of flowers, the lullaby of music, the glittering of stars, the rainbow after a storm—all these and more tell us that God wants us to have joy and have it in abundance.

G. K. Chesterton wrote, "Man is more himself . . . when joy is the fundamental thing in him, and grief the superficial."[73] His words reflect Our Lord's message:

Amen, amen, I say to you, . . . you will grieve, but your grief will become joy. When a woman is in labor, she is in anguish because her hour has arrived; but when she has given birth to a child, she no longer remembers the pain because of her joy that a child has been born into the world. So you also are now in anguish. But I will see you again, and your hearts will rejoice, and no one will take your joy away from you. (John 16:20-22)

Like the pain of labor, our suffering will bring about new life. Would our loved one, who now lives in the constant joy of heaven, want us to continue to walk in sorrow? Surely they want us to have joy and might even be trying to sprinkle it down upon us. Let's open our hearts to the little bits of joy that float around us every day.

Turning from grief to joy must be a deliberate decision. God will lead us there, but we must be willing to make the choice to put aside our grief. God won't rip it from our shoulders.

Laughing Again

Allowing ourselves to laugh is part of the process of letting joy back into our lives. We've considered Matthew's version of the beatitudes: "Blessed are they who mourn, / for they will be comforted" (5:4). The Evangelist Luke records slightly different wording: "Blessed are you who are now weeping, / for you will laugh" (Luke 6:21).

Laughter is good for us. It releases stress hormones. It makes us feel better. It truly is the best medicine. My brother's eulogy for my dad was full of comedy that made us laugh together at the most difficult time. He made us feel good.

God made me laugh the night we were told there was nothing more they could do for Dad. He was dying. When I got into my car in the dark hospital parking lot, the radio came on, blasting the words of a popular Christian song, "Home." Vocal artist Chris Tomlin sang of going home to a place where every tear is wiped away and the streets are paved in gold, going to a place where he knew he belonged. Suddenly the tears I had been holding back all day were released in a flood. The reality hit me: I was losing my dad. He too was going home. I sobbed uncontrollably. But in the midst of my tears, I heard myself laughing—laughing because I knew my great God had sent me this song, at this exact moment, to assure me that all would be well.

Sometimes we may laugh spontaneously during the worst days of death and farewell. But then we feel guilty and spend weeks or months suppressing our laughter and our joy. St. Paul tells us, "The fruit of the Spirit is love, joy, peace. . . . Against such there is no law" (Galatians 5:22, 23). *There is no law against joy!!* Nowhere in the world is there a law that says we cannot be happy, we cannot laugh, or we cannot live in joy after a loved one has died. When we refuse joy, we impose a heavy burden on ourselves, and it's a burden we ourselves must lift.

We need to ask ourselves, "How long have we been chained to grief? Have we forgotten how to smile? Do we refuse to allow ourselves to have a good time? Have we covered all the doors and windows of our hearts and blocked out even the slightest glimmer of joy?" This is no way to live. Psychologists say that those who do not take time for joy, laughter, and good times are setting themselves up for grave physical and mental problems. We must open the door to joy. We must laugh again.

The Old Testament priest Ezra says, "Today is holy to our Lord. Do not be saddened this day, for rejoicing in the Lord is your strength!" (Nehemiah 8:10). When we're willing to let joy and laughter back into our lives, we'll find the strength to let go of our sadness. We'll be able to rejoice in the Lord and feel that our days are good and holy.

Closer to Heaven

The Liturgy of the Hours, also known as the Divine Office, is the official daily prayer of the Church. Ordained and consecrated people must pray the Hours or some portion of it daily, and many laypeople choose to pray it as well. The Liturgy of the Hours is a collection of ever-changing prayers, Scripture, and nonbiblical readings, said throughout the day, marking certain hours of the day. One prayer in this collection, however, is fairly constant. It is the first prayer of the morning, the Venite Exsultemus Domino, or the Venite. It begins,

> Come, let us sing joyfully to the LORD;
> > cry out to the rock of our salvation.
> Let us come before him with a song of praise,
> > joyfully sing out our psalms.
> For the LORD is the great God,
> > the great king over all gods,
> Whose hand holds the depths of the earth;
> > who owns the tops of the mountains. (Psalm 95:1-4)

Every day, all around the world, the first prayer on millions of lips is a prayer for joy. This is how important joy is.

This prayer also tells us that God can be found on the tops of mountains. When we began our grief journey, we were in the dark valley. And yes, God was there too, in the mists and the depths. But the view is so much better from the top of a mountain. It is there that we can really find joy. Let us climb that mountain. Mountains, after all, are just a little closer to heaven than deep valleys.

Jesus often took his followers to the top of a mountain when he wanted to teach them something significant. He was transfigured on top of a mountain. He taught us the beatitudes on top of a mountain, affirming that those who mourn will be comforted. And he said his farewell to us atop a mountain. He promised, "Behold, I am with you always, until the end of the age" (Matthew 28:20).

We might think having Jesus always with us should guarantee constant joy. But as spiritual writer Henri Nouwen says, "Joy does not simply happen to us. We have to choose joy and keep choosing it every day."[74] This advice is everywhere. "Choose Joy" appears on coffee mugs, wall plaques, pillows, T-shirts, necklaces, and even tattoos. Why are constant reminders to choose joy so important for us? Henri Nouwen offers an explanation. "Joy is always new. Whereas there can be old pain, old grief, and old sorrow, there can be no old joy. Old joy is not joy! Joy is always connected with movement, renewal, rebirth, change—in short, with life."[75]

How do we find this fresh new joy every day? "Consider it all joy," St. James suggests (1:2). Our faith has been tested by grief. But God is with us still. We are closer to heaven now because someone we love resides there. Yet life on earth is moving forward, and we need to move with it. New things, good things, are waiting. Let us indeed "consider it all joy."

Try This

Embrace the dawn. Scripture says,

> At dusk weeping comes for the night;
>> but at dawn there is rejoicing. (Psalm 30:6)

Dawn happens on even the stormiest days, though we might not see it. Dawn lights up the clearest mornings. Dawn is often most beautiful when there are some clouds in the sky to reflect the rays of the sun. So it is in your life. Even though some clouds of grief may linger, they can make the joys of your life even lovelier and more appreciated.

If you happen to be outside right before dawn, you will hear birds beginning to sing. Let your heart sing with them. Plan time to sit and watch the dawn whenever you can. Weather apps will tell you the exact time of dawn where you are. If you cannot experience the actual dawn on a regular basis, find a lovely image of dawn to remind you that God always offers us a new day, a new joy. Take the gift he offers, and cherish it.

Wanting Joy

Dear Lord,
I want joy in my life again.
I am weary of the tears and sadness.
Yet still I cry as you did,
"The spirit is willing, but the flesh is weak" (Matthew 26:41).
My spirit is hungry for your joy,
but my flesh still longs for the one I have lost.
I don't want you to bring them back to me.
That would be so selfish.
I wouldn't take away their heavenly joy for anything.
So I ask you, please, to help me find joy right now in
earthly blessings.
Help me laugh and sing again.
Help me climb out of the dark valley and enjoy life from
the mountaintop,
where the view is better, and I can be close to you.
Help me welcome every dawn with a heart open to
new joy.
Renew my life, and let me embrace all its beauty
and goodness.
I open my arms to receive your precious gift of joy.
Thank you, great and wonderful Father. Amen.

Notes

1. St. Elizabeth Ann Seton, quoted in Anne Merwin, *Elizabeth Ann Seton* (Boston: Pauline Books and Media, 2015), 36-37.
2. Unites States Conference of Catholic Bishops, *United States Catholic Catechism for Adults* (Washington, D.C.: USCCB, 2006), 3.
3. C. S. Lewis, *A Grief Observed* (Project Gutenberg Canada: Ebook Samizdat, 2016), 1, 35.
4. St. Elizabeth Ann Seton, quoted in Merwin, 62-63.
5. Lewis, 31.
6. St. Ephrem, quoted by Fr. Joe Kempf, *No One Cries the Wrong Way* (Huntington, IN: Our Sunday Visitor, 2012), 11.
7. Thérèse of Lisieux, *The Story of a Soul: The Autobiography of the Little Flower* (Charlotte, NC: St. Benedict Press, 2010), 43.
8. Eucharistic Prayer I, *Roman Missal*.
9. Eucharistic Prayer II, *Roman Missal*.
10. Eucharistic Prayer IV, *Roman Missal*.
11. Pope Francis, *Evangelii Gaudium* [Apostolic Exhortation on the Proclamation of the Gospel in the Today's World], November 24, 2013, 47, http://w2.vatican.va/content/francesco/en/apost_exhortations/documents/papa-francesco_esortazione-ap_20131124_evangelii-gaudium.html#_ftnref51.
12. Ibid., 113.
13. Pope Francis, *Gaudete et Exsultate* [Apostolic Exhortation on the Call to Holiness in Today's World], March 19, 2018, 114 http://w2.vatican.va/content/francesco/en/apost_exhortations/documents/papa-francesco_esortazione-ap_20180319_gaudete-et-exsultate.html.

14. See G. K. Chesterton, *The Everlasting Man* (San Francisco: Ignatius, 1993), part 1, chapter 4, "God and Comparative Religion."

15. Thomas à Kempis, *The Imitation of Christ* (Notre Dame, IN: Ave Maria Press, 2017), 154.

16. Ibid, 169.

17. Teresa of Ávila, quoted by Elizabeth A Dreyer, *Accidental Theologians: Four Women Who Shaped Christianity* (Cincinnati: Franciscan Media, 2014), 85.

18. Pope St. John XXIII, *Journal of a Soul: The Autobiography of Pope John XXIII* (New York: Image Books, 1999), 30, 41.

19. Ibid., 12.

20. Thérèse of Lisieux, 19.

21. Anne Morrow Lindbergh, https://www.goodreads.com/quotes/611246-it-isn-t-for-the-moment-you-are-stuck-that-you.

22. Lindbergh, https://www.azquotes.com/author/8886-Anne_Morrow_Lindbergh.

23. Lindbergh, www.goodreads.com/work/quotes/37467-gift-from-the-sea.

24. St. Elizabeth Ann Seton, quoted in Merwin, 13.

25. Inscription on the Memorial of the SeaBees, US Naval Construction Battalions, http://www.anvari.org/fortune/Miscellaneous_Collections/408726_the-difficult-we-do-today-the-impossible-takes-a-little-longer.html.

26. Pope Francis, *Evangelii Gaudium,* 3.

27. Lindbergh, *Gift from the Sea,* https://www.goodreads.com/quotes/25569-i-do-not-believe-that-sheer-suffering-teaches-if-suffering.

28. Pope Francis, *Misericordiae Vultus* [Bull of Indiction of the Extraordinary Jubilee of Mercy], April 11, 2015, 9, https://w2.vatican.va/content/francesco/en/apost_letters/documents/papa-francesco_bolla_20150411_misericordiae-vultus.html.

29. Ibid., 3.

30. *United States Catholic Catechism for Adults,* 173.

31. Pope St. John XXIII, 47, 48, 49.

32. A Kempis, 207.

33. Prayer of Padre Pio after Communion, https://padrepiodevotions.org/wp-content/uploads/2013/01/padre-pio-prayer-sheet.pdf.

34. James Martin, *Between Heaven and Mirth: Why Joy, Humor, and Laughter Are at the Heart of the Spiritual Life* (New York: Harper One, 2012), 87.

35. Lewis, 36, 20.

36. Cf. Council of Florence (1439); DS 1304; Council of Trent (1563): DS 1820; (1547): 1580; see also Benedict XII, *Benedictus Deus* (1336): DS 1000.

37. *United States Catholic Catechism for Adults*, 160.

38. Pope St. John XXIII, 53, 250.

39. Pope Francis, *Gaudete et Exsultate,* 14.

40. Ibid., 63.

41. Ibid., 75, 76.

42. Pope Francis, *Evangelii Gaudium,* 71.

43. C. S. Lewis, *The Four Loves* (New York: HarperCollins, 2017), 176.

44. Thérèse of Lisieux, 17.

45. Ibid.

46. Ibid., 53, 54.

47. Pope St. John Paul II, *Rosarium Virginis Mariae,* [Apostolic Letter on the Most Holy Rosary], October 16, 2002, 40, https://w2.vatican.va/content/john-paul-ii/en/apost_letters/2002/documents/hf_jp-ii_apl_20021016_rosarium-virginis-mariae.html.

48. Sr. Maria Lucia of Jesus and the Immaculate Heart, https://aleteia.org/2017/02/16/7-powerful-quotes-from-fatima-visionary-sister-lucia/.

49. Pope Francis, *Urbi et Orbi* Message [To the City and to the World], March 31, 2013, http://w2.vatican.va/content/francesco/en/messages/urbi/documents/papa-francesco_20130331_urbi-et-orbi-pasqua.html.

50. Thomas Merton, *The New Man* (New York: Farrar, Straus & Giroux, 1961), 242.

51. *United States Catholic Catechism for Adults*, 333.

52. Fr. Pierre Teilhard de Chardin, "Patient Trust," quoted in Michael Harter, SJ, ed., *Hearts on Fire: Praying with Jesuits* (Chicago: Loyola Press, 2005), 102-103.

53. Pope St. John XXIII, Daily Decalogue, 1, 10, http://www.appleseeds.org/Decalogue_John-23.htm.

54. Thérèse of Lisieux, 80.

55. St. Basil the Great, https://www.goodreads.com/ quotes/354699-when-someone-steals-another-s-clothes-we -call-them-a-thief.

56. Pope St. John XXIII, 48.

57. Pope Francis, *Laudato Si'* [Encyclical on Care for Our Common Home], May 24, 2015, 222, http://w2.vatican .va/content/francesco/en/encyclicals/documents/papa -francesco_20150524_enciclica-laudato-si.html.

58. Thomas of Celano, quoted by John Michael Talbot, *The Lessons of St. Francis: How to Bring Simplicity and Spirituality into Your Daily Life* (New York: Penguin Group, 1997), 26.

59. Pope Francis, *Gaudete et Exsultate*, 56.

60. Ibid., 104, 107.

61. Ibid., 76.

62. Mother Teresa, *Come Be My Light: The Private Writings of the Saint of Calcutta,* ed. Brian Kolodiejchuk, MC (New York: Doubleday, 2009), 281.

63. Pope Francis, *Gaudete et Exsultate,* 136.

64. Mary Shelley, *Frankenstein* (Ayra Publishing: Pandora's Box Classics, Kindle Edition, 2018), 8.

65. Elisabeth Kübler-Ross, http://www.wiseoldsayings.com/ authors/elisabeth-kubler-ross-quotes/.

66. Saint Teresa of Avila, www.inconversion.wordpress.com.

67. Catherine of Siena, quoted in Dreyer, 54.

68. St. Augustine, Sermon 169, 11, 13: PL 38, 923.

69. Thérèse of Lisieux, 99.

70. Lewis, *A Grief Observed*, 21.

71. St. Elizabeth Ann Seton, quoted in Merwin, 12.

72. A Kempis, 218.

73. G. K. Chesterton, quoted in Dale Ahlquist, *Way of Wonder: Wisdom from G. K. Chesterton* (Boston: Pauline Books and Media, 2016), 113.

74. Henri Nouwen, https://www.goodreads.com/quotes/396401-joy-does-not-simply-happen-to-us-we-have-to.

75. Henry Nouwen, quoted in Michael Ford, ed., *Eternal Seasons: A Liturgical Journey with Henri J. M. Nouwen* (Notre Dame, IN: Sorin Books, 2004), 127.

theWORD
among us®
The *Spirit* of Catholic Living

This book was published by The Word Among Us. Since 1981, The Word Among Us has been answering the call of the Second Vatican Council to help Catholic laypeople encounter Christ in the Scriptures.

The name of our company comes from the prologue to the Gospel of John and reflects the vision and purpose of all of our publications: to be an instrument of the Spirit, whose desire is to manifest Jesus' presence in and to the children of God. In this way, we hope to contribute to the Church's ongoing mission of proclaiming the gospel to the world so that all people would know the love and mercy of our Lord and grow more deeply in their faith as missionary disciples.

Our monthly devotional magazine, *The Word Among Us*, features meditations on the daily and Sunday Mass readings and currently reaches more than one million Catholics in North America and another half-million Catholics in one hundred countries around the world. Our book division, The Word Among Us Press, publishes numerous books, Bible studies, and pamphlets that help Catholics grow in their faith.

To learn more about who we are and what we publish, visit us at www.wau.org. There you will find a variety of Catholic resources that will help you grow in your faith.

Embrace His Word, Listen to God . . .

www.wau.org